Call Center Essentials

A Practical Guide to Real-Time Results

Call Center Essentials

A Practical Guide to Real-Time Results

Chitra G. Lele

ATLANTIC

PUBLISHERS & DISTRIBUTORS (P) LTD

Published by

ATLANTIC

PUBLISHERS & DISTRIBUTORS (P) LTD

7/22, Ansari Road, Darya Ganj,
New Delhi-110002
Phones: +91-11-40775252, 23273880, 23275880, 23280451
Fax : +91-11-23285873
Web : www.atlanticbooks.com
E-mail : orders@atlanticbooks.com

Branch Office
5, Nallathambi Street, Wallajah Road,
Chennai-600002
Phones: +91-44-64611085, 32413319
E-mail : chennai@atlanticbooks.com

ISBN 978-81-269-1797-6

Printed in India at Nice Printing Press, A-33/3A, Site-IV, Industrial Area, Sahibabad, Ghaziabad, U.P.

Printed in India at Glorious Printers, A-13, D.S.I.D.C., Jhilmil Industrial Area, Delhi-110095

Dedication

My mother, whose support and love
Have kept me going always;
Words will never be able to describe
What she means to me!

Customer Satisfaction
And Loyalty
Lead to
Lasting Success.

Culture of Caring
Enhances
Net Sales,
Track Record,
Experience Management and
Return on Investment.

—Chitra G. Lele

To serve is to rule.

—Chinese Proverb

Foreword–I

I am delighted to write the foreword for the book written by the young and accomplished author, Chitra G. Lele. *Call Center Essentials: A Practical Guide to Real-Time Results* is a highly comprehensive guide to call center operations. Call centers represent one of the fastest growing and most important sources of service employment, particularly in India, as witnessed by the huge growth of these centers outsourced there from around the world. While call centers have become the subject of considerable scholarship for research into work and organizations over recent years, limited practical guidance has been available until now for those wishing to improve call center operations, whether they are managing or training in a call center or are in the process of setting up new operations.

Although the character of call center operations often varies, typically a key operational aim is increasing customer throughput while reducing service delivery costs. This is where this book will prove useful, given its focus on providing a practical guide to real-time results.

Written in an engaging and lively style, the book covers a range of topics, right from the micro perspective of 'getting started in a call center' through to the macro perspective of the 'future in India'. Chitra has divided the subject matter into four different parts, which can be read independently of each other providing an 'easy to follow' structure for the reader.

Part 1: "From the Ground Up—Getting Started" is a 'back to basics' consideration of call centers, their evolution, rationale for growth, main functions and accompanying changes in technologies from basic systems to the contemporary multichannel, multiservice real-time entities. In addition to providing background for the reader, this section will enable them to identify where their own particular call center fits along the call center continuum.

Part 2: "Staying On the Path—Customer Experience Excellence" emphasizes the need to develop a customer-oriented approach and the influence of agents on the customer experience. Chitra explains that one way of doing this is to create processes and models that enable superior performance measurement and management, thus allowing call centers to stay ahead of the competition.

Part 3: "Call Centers in India—The First Choice" explains why organizations around the world choose India for their outsourced call center services in comparison to other Asian nations. Given predictions are that growth in India will continue for some considerable time, then those readers who are currently either in the process of improving operations or setting up call centers in India will be able to benefit from this book.

Part 4: "Fast Forward—Be Future-Ready" includes real-life insights, scenarios and success stories from call center personnel, which help to illustrate organizational effectiveness in call center operations. The section also considers trends and speculations concerning the future of these centers as well as potential adaptations and marketing approaches.

Integral to the book is Chitra's unique theory, 'The Wheel of Nurture', which is a novel combination of management principles and human factors encompassing customers, tools, performance and communication in call centers. Moreover, her book provides resources and a wide range of information and tools designed to assist with recruiting and retaining the appropriate personnel, product development and location sourcing for such centers with the goal of assisting with the maximization of business gains and return on investment.

The proposed readership for this book includes call center consultants, ranging from managers and frontline staff supervisors to trainers and customer service representatives, whether new or experienced in call center operations. The book would also be useful for teachers and students involved in call center education.

Whatever your background and experience, I hope you both enjoy reading the book and benefit from its academic content.

Dr. Julia Connell,
Professor of Management,
Co-Director—Change, People and
Organisational Wellbeing
Research Cluster,
Curtin University, Australia

Note

Professor Connell has published numerous conference papers and journal articles related to call centers and call center operations as well as two edited editions:

Burgess, J. and Connell, J. (2004), *Emerging Developments in Call Centre Research, Labour and Industry* (published April).

Burgess, J. & Connell, J. (Eds), (2006) *International Developments in the Call Centre Industry: Analysis, Policy and Challenges,* Routledge: London.

Foreword–II

Chitra G. Lele's book, *Call Center Essentials: A Practical Guide to Real-Time Results,* is essential and easy reading for those who seek employment in a call center, either as a customer service representative (CSR), as a supervisor or as a manager. For those at the entry level, this book introduces the jargon of the industry and to a philosophy which, if adopted, should position them well for employment in the industry. It certainly provides all of the information that will enable you to differentiate yourself from the many thousands of willing but less informed applicants. It also provides benchmarks against which you can compare potential employers (assuming you have a choice about where you obtain employment). Once employed, the time you will need to feel competent and able to make a strong contribution to your new business should be shortened if you have worked your way through the book with care. You will know about what good service looks and sounds like, so your service levels should be high, and this should be recognized early with appropriate rewards by your employers. Another advantage of this book is that it provides guidance on how to ensure your well-being while at work—an often overlooked issue in call centers. For supervisors, the terrain is well covered and there is much guidance here for their role as well. Human resource development officers might find that this book is a worthwhile investment for all new staff. If you have come to the call center industry from another area of business, you will also find the book invaluable. Checklists are provided for those thinking of setting up a call center with practical advice that many may have overlooked in their planning.

Clearly India is the key hub of the world's call centers, and whilst it once had a reputation of simply being cheap, its reputation is moving to being much more. The industry as well as the level of offshore outsourcing from western countries appears to have increased dramatically, and I am reliably informed that one no longer can just outsource established proven processes to Indian call centers but that the level of sophistication is such that "broken processes" and less than effective processes can often be made effective by the sophistication and talent in Indian call centers. Although I have previously argued that call centers are so important to the success of a business that outsourcing call center operations tantamount to a lack of concern for customers, and the operations of many call centers would still have me believe that this can still be the case, yet outsourcing to a technologically sophisticated operation that is well managed may at times be much better than that can be provided in-house or in-country, especially to provide a cost-effective 24 hour provision of service.

As a customer, though, one never really knows whether you are calling the business directly or an outsourced provider for the business but, whoever it is, the level of service reflects on the brand of the business. As pointed out by Chitra, the onus of responsibility on the CSR is high and the time in which to achieve a perception of added value is short. I am confident that the adoption of many of the techniques suggested here will lead to a higher level of service in the industry.

Professor Lynne Bennington,
Services Management Consultant,
University Professor (Faculty of Business, ACU, Melbourne, Australia) and Co-author (with Professor Richard Feinberg, a consumer psychologist, and Professor Ko de Ruyter, a marketing expert) of the 2005 publication
Cases in Call Center Management: Great Ideas (Th)at Work, Purdue University Press

Introduction

The manager who is doing exactly what he/she was doing 12 months ago will not survive with the expediential changes we are all experiencing now and over the next decade. *Call Center Essentials: A Practical Guide to Real-Time Results* seeks to provide a comprehensive and realistic blueprint for delivering top-of-the-class customer experiences across channels, which the young author, Chitra Lele, aptly refers to as 'Customer EDGExperiences'.

In the rapidly changing and advancing world of customer contact never has it been more important to raise the bar to improve customer and employee experience and deliver *more with less*. All customer contact practitioners in the 21st century need to ask themselves three important questions:

1. Is the customer truly at the center of how we think, behave and perform, and what can be done to differentiate and optimize customer experiences through integration of social media, new technologies and innovation?
2. Are my organization, my operations and my teams consistently demonstrating real value and return on investment in customer contact?
3. How is the employee experience being improved to attract and retain brilliant people from the frontline to the boardroom?

Today's customer contact leaders not only need to develop robust customer experience strategies and deliver bottom line results—they also need to drive change. Keeping up-to-date, generating new ideas and ensuring smooth implementation in a dynamic, fast-moving world is exactly where this book will help. It provides a practical roadmap with great signposts for improvement across all the operational aspects of call center performance, right from recruitment, training, tools and technologies, operations management, people and processes through to quality and productivity, and above all, delivering personalized, immersive, consistent customer experiences, whilst achieving operational excellence.

Chitra Lele is a very determined author with a passion to share her knowledge, ideas and expertise. This how-to-essentials guide will definitely help managers to shape and adapt call centers to the future.

Natalie Calvert,
Chief Executive Officer, Calcomgroup.com and
Editor, *Gower Handbook of Call and Contact Centre Management*
nataliecalvert@twitter.com

Preface

"We will be with you as soon as possible", "Kindly be on line", or "Your call is important to us". Do these lines sound familiar? Well, most everyone has heard them and they mainly emanate from a call center. Making a call to ask for technical help or to order a product has become a part and parcel of our lives. In today's business landscape, it is rare to find an industry that does not require call centers; they are a key asset to each and every business entity.

Today, the term 'call center' is practically a household name. Chances are that you are holding *Call Center Essentials: A Practical Guide to Real-Time Results* because you are managing, training or setting up a call center. This book takes you behind the scenes and helps you make the most out of your investment to build a real-time profit center.

Today, the customers expect to have not just great products and services, but also superior call center experiences, something I refer to as 'Customer EDGExperience'. The main focus of my book is to help call centers in delivering these Customer EDGExperiences, and in building, maintaining and eventually increasing the lifetime value of an organization's relationship with the customer base. The book provides comprehensive resources to find the right personnel, the right products, the right tools and a whole gamut of the right call center-related factors.

This book is divided into four parts, each with its own unique focus. Part 1 covers the foundation topics like history, definitions, types, applications and outsourcing options of call centers. This part deals with how and why call centers are described as learning organizations. It also dwells on important topics like human factors, site selection aspects and career avenues. Part 2 describes my unique theory of superior customer-focused experiences—*The Wheel of Nurture*; this theory is a novel combination of management principles and human factors. It deals with the CARE formula and experience drivers, which provide the personal touch and human insights to overhaul customer experience management. It also discusses the supporting factors for the theory in terms of customers, tools, performance and communication. Part 3 covers the history of call centers in India, reasons for their phenomenal growth in India and how this growth has catapulted India to a higher economic status. Aspects like the current status of call centers in India and India's position in comparison with other competing nations are also dealt with in this part. Major emerging trends and forecasts of the Indian call center space are covered in the last chapter of this part. Part 4 contains real-life insights of industry experts and professionals. This part also explores new horizons, what must be done by call centers to prepare for the customers of tomorrow and what are the likely global trends that call centers will witness in the future. Appendix A shares details of some of the leading business and industry associations that promote and support call centers. Appendix B lists a number of useful resources on call centers.

The audience for this book is all types of call center professionals, right from the call center managers and supervisors to trainers and customer service representatives. This book contains doable nuggets for both novices and experts. It will be useful for the following:

1. Top management, front-line managers, supervisors, training managers, consultants and call center representatives of an already established call center.
2. Organizations that are either going to build a call center from scratch or outsource their operations.
3. Teachers, students and all those interested in understanding call center dynamics.

Whether you are a team leader, manager, supervisor or coach, you play a crucial role in the success of your call center—*Leadership*. Whether you are a call center representative or trainee, you play an important function in the customer contact cycle—*Emotional Intelligence*. This book contains practicable advice to perform these roles and functions flawlessly.

All the tools needed to facilitate quick understanding are provided—figures and tables that clarify concepts, spotlight tips, useful worksheets, real-life insights, easy-to-use checklists, illustrations that highlight the realities of the call center world in an intellectually stimulating manner, and much more.

My hope is to spark new intellectual thoughts and ideas. Dive right in and learn about call center dynamics!

Chitra G. Lele

Acknowledgements

I take this opportunity to express my thanks to those who have helped me directly or indirectly in writing this book.

First and foremost, special thanks go to my parents, Mrs. Asha Lele and Mr. G.G. Lele, for being my inspiration and for believing in me. This book is the result of their initiative and whole-hearted support. I dedicate this book to them.

I give my sincere thanks to God for being my guide and helping me along the way in so many mysterious ways.

I am grateful to Dr. Julia Connell whose guidance, encouragement and support, right from the initial to the final stage, enabled me to complete the book successfully. I thank her for writing a scholarly Foreword–I for the book.

I owe my deepest gratitude to Ms. Lynne Bennington for her scholarly Foreword–II, useful feedback, and continued mentorship.

I would like to express my special gratitude and thanks to Ms. Natalie Calvert for her kind cooperation and encouragement and for sparing time to write a wonderful Introduction to the book.

Without the comprehensive research studies conducted by several premier market research firms, sharing of vital research findings, valuable actionable insights and market trends would not have been possible. Many thanks to these firms for their relentless efforts in keeping us abreast of the latest developments on the call center horizon.

Very special thanks go out to the members of the Brainlines Team (www.brainlines.net) for their excellent creative work on the illustrations.

It is due to the unstinted help of various call center professionals and experts whom I met across the globe that I am able to share so many valuable insights with you all.

I thank all the contributors of the "Real Life Insights—Through the Eyes of an Expert" chapter. It is because of these thorough professionals that we get to learn interesting facts and trends of call centers. I am grateful to these experts for their thought-provoking experiences and illuminating discussions.

Last but not least, I am extremely thankful to my publishers, Atlantic Publishers and Distributors. The steadfast support, constructive comments and ceaseless cooperation from the Atlantic team are thankfully acknowledged.

Chitra G. Lele

Contents

PART 4: FAST FORWARD—BE FUTURE-READY

APPENDICES

List of Tables, Illustrations, Figures, Worksheets and Checklists

A. List of Tables

B. List of Illustrations

C. List of Figures

D. List of Worksheets

E. List of Checklists

PART-I

From the Ground Up—Getting Started

In this part...

Foundation topics like the history, types, definitions, applications and outsourcing options of call centers are covered.

This part deals with how and why call centers are described as learning organizations.

It also dwells on important topics like human factors, site selection aspects and career avenues in call centers.

Introduction—Call Centers are the Face of Organizations

1

Providing high-quality customer experiences is important both for today and the future, and call centers are the *nucleus* of all this action. They are the primary touch point and the *epicenter of customer experiences*. Right from carrying out transactions over the rotary dial telephones to their modern-day avatar of web-enabled integrated call management and intelligent digital networks, call centers have built up quite a rich history for themselves. They are a vital link between businesses and the customers. Call centers are the face, voice and ears of an organization; they can make or mar the corporate image of an organization in the market.

New trends come and go, but customer service can never go out of style. Today's call centers are beginning to move beyond their traditional role of just performing customer service. They are more focused on identifying and implementing new winning strategies of taking this service to the next level of performance, integrating technology with the sales and marketing resources, and designing their offerings to fit the various customer channels.

1.1 History—The Revolutionary Evolution

What began with the shifting of manufacturing goods to countries providing cheap labor during the Industrial Revolution, has taken a completely revolutionary road on today's information superhighway.

Carrying out business transactions over the telephone has a long history. The toll-free services and the invention of Automatic Call Distributor (ACD) made call centers possible. The toll-free service (introduced in 1960s) is a free telecommunication service that allows the customers to connect to organizations without incurring toll charges. As toll-free became popular, organizations began finding innovative ways of using this service, one of which is the central theme of this book—*Call Centers*. Another precursor to call centers is ACD. ACD is a specialized system that recognizes, answers and routes incoming calls to customer service representatives (CSRs) based on a routing strategy; ACD made handling a greater number of calls in an efficient manner possible. A CSR is an individual who provides customer service or sells a product via telephone or other contact channels in a call center environment. Other titles for a CSR include call center agent, contact center representative, sales or service representative and many more. We will be using the terms CSR and agent interchangeably in this book.

It all started with operator services followed with reservation lines (particularly for the airlines industry) and catalog ordering centers. One of the widely known earlier ACD installation was developed in 1973 by a US firm named Rockwell International. This installation was designed to handle the telephone booking operations of Continental Airlines. There is evidence that the basic functionality of call centers was in action more than a decade before Rockwell. Some of the early players in this space were the Manchester Evening News in 1970 and Barclaycard in 1972. Some of the major call centers of the 1980s were Direct Line—UK's first telephone insurer launched in 1985 and First Direct—UK's first telephone bank launched in 1989. In USA, Aspect Telecommunications was a major player.

Before the mid-1970s, phone rooms were used for dealing with the customer calls; phone rooms—the precursor to the modern-day call centers. Earlier, manufacturing organizations were predominant players. Previously, it was all about telephone traffic statistics, but with technology and the emergence of the dotcom customers, it is about providing prompt services and consistent experiences now. As organizations have become aware that customer-focused experiences are the key to expanding business, the common (mis)conception about call centers has changed.

Initially, call center operations were limited to operator services and reservations, but with the outsourcing boom, technological revolution, globalization, techniques to communicate complex information through various mediums in real-time, cost-containment pressures, and the recent rise of social media like blogs, microblogs, social networking sites, etc., the customer needs have expanded exponentially. And this is exactly the reason why call centers are not mere call-taking departments anymore, but are a fully operational extension of businesses with massive customer service operations.

Call centers have evolved over the years to do much more than just answer telephone calls. Now, we enjoy the benefits of several types of call center services due to the phenomenal advances in telecommunication, digital exchanges and Information Technology. Over the last two decades or so, the high rate at which the customers and calls have grown, it was necessary for organizations to upgrade their service delivery models to provide multi-channel customer service and support.

These days, almost every organization that deals in products and services, needs call centers to provide customer support. The growth of call centers has propelled the growth of the world economy. From their days of modest beginnings of basic computer support to the multi-billion dollar, web-enabled service industry, call centers have come a long way. No wonder, they have contributed in more ways than one to the service industry. Insurance, Travel, Retail Banking, Finance and many more—you name it and you have a call center for it. Even non-profit organizations use the services of a call center to promote their causes. Many a time, there are organizations that need the services of a call center for a one-time event, for example, a special function where the services of a call center are needed to send out invitations to people. These examples speak volumes of the all-pervasive nature of call centers.

The geographical spread of call centers has opened up the gateway of opportunities for many new nations like India, China, Canada, etc. These countries have experienced a tremendous growth rate in call centers in the last 8-10 years as large players like the USA and UK outsource their back-office activities to these countries due to substantial time and cost savings. Coupled with this spread is the emergence of call centers in several new outsourcing options like research process outsourcing, legal process outsourcing, knowledge process outsourcing, etc.

In the early 1990s, organizations only outsourced jobs to some of the local organizations that offered the services they were looking for, but in the mid-1990s when the first wave of technology combined with globalization and the precipitous rise of the Internet hit the global shores, call centers began to burgeon on a world-wide scale. Another reason for the spread of call centers in the 1990s was retrenchment in various sectors and the cost-cutting drive taken up by several organizations. Despite the 'dot com' boom and its subsequent burst, call centers continued to grow. The early 2000s witnessed further growth in call centers through the trend of offshore outsourcing. Offshore outsourcing is the practice of sending certain types of business operations like IT/ITES work, healthcare, etc., overseas, which is handled by an external organization/independent third party.

The combined power of the Internet and E-Business led to the introduction of new service channels in the mid-1990s. Call centers with the ability to deal with the customers through channels like e-mail, chat, voice mail and paging, etc., began to be introduced. This is when the call centers began to shift from hardware-dependent solutions to software-centric solutions.

Today, call centers are even heralded as a source of women liberation and economic freedom as there is a large number of women working in call centers. Call centers provide women employees a chance to prove their mettle in the global economy.

The modern-day concept of call centers has undertaken a completely new image and has undergone a major scope creep rather a major revolution. Nowadays, call centers are also referred to as Contact Centers as they handle a mix of customer transactions—both traditional (Telephone calls) and modern (Fax, E-Mail, Web Chat, Voice-Mail, etc). The call center globe is being orbited by millions of such multichannel-driven customer calls.

Illustration 1.1: The Call Center Globe is being Orbited by Millions of Multichannel-driven Customer Calls

> **Spotlight Tip**
>
> The shift in platforms and technologies shows that call centers are swiftly evolving. Today, organizations build their businesses around call center capability.

You will find an advertisement with a smiling face and a headset, and with a promising message of great service, in every nook and corner. There is hardly a week that goes by without buzz related to call centers. Today, organizations view call centers as an excellent opportunity to focus on their customers and really grow their businesses. Call centers are a fascinating trend in themselves.

1.1.1 Definition—Much More Than the Name

The person who called you two days ago with details of a new insurance scheme—called from a...call center. Last week my friend called a toll-free number to check on the status of her book order—the place where her call was received is a...call center.

Defining call centers is not a simple task. There are several definitions available in the call center literature—some simple, some complex, some narrow and some broad. Let us have a look at some of the important definitions here.

The traditional definition of a call center describes call centers as a place where business is done by phone; a place where calls are answered or made. But today it is much more than that. As time went by, call center definitions took on more meaning; they became much more diverse in nature and technology is constantly redefining them.

One early definition described call centers as a place of doing business by phone that combined a centralized database with an automated call distribution system.

The broadest definition is coined by Norling, who states that "a call centre is any communications platform from which firms deliver services to customers via remote, real-time contact".

The definition given by the *Macmillan Dictionary* defines call centers as "A place where a large number of people are employed to deal with customers by telephone, either in order to sell something or to answer questions".

The *PC Magazine Encyclopedia* defines a call center as "A department within a company or a third-party organization that handles telephone sales and/or service".

The British Call Center Association (1999) defines a call center as follows "a physical or virtual operation within an organization in which a managed group of people spend most of their time doing business by telephone, usually working in a computer automated setting".

In another frequently cited definition, Richardson (1994) states that "telephone call centers are specialist technology-intensive offices that are established by organizations in order to deliver services to customers over the telephone, replacing or complementing face-to-face interaction with the public". This same definition holds true for any other channel of customer contact; we expand it to include the newer modes of customer contact channels like E-Mail, Fax, Websites and Mobile Phones.

Present-day call centers cater to a gamut of industries like Retail, Manufacturing, Utility, Public Sector and many more, and encompass diverse functions of these industries like billing, crisis management, software setup and maintenance, claims processing and many more. Some call them help desks, some call them processing centers, some refer to them as customer hot lines and some refer to them as customer service centers.

From the above definitions, we can conclude the following key points about call centers:

A. A call center is a place, either a physical facility or a virtual setup, where customer service or customer care is the primary concern.

B. A call center is much more than just a location for taking and making calls. It is an umbrella term that covers a host of applications and business functions for a host of industries.

C. A call center is a highly specialized functional facility housed within an organization or is an outsourced, separate unit.

D. A call center is a means to form and encourage new business relationships by tapping into new customer segments, for example, acquiring new customers who use new modes of communication channels like social networking and smart phones.

E. A call center performs its operations through integrated telephone and information technologies.

F. Over the last few years, the common perception of a call center has changed.

G. A call center is the catalyst for corporate change.

H. Today, call centers are an integral part of local and global economies.

1.2 Reasons for Growth—The Cynosure of World-Wide Attention

Call centers have grown at a fast rate over the last couple of years. In the current age of technology-intensive workplaces and internet marketing, it is possible to offer advanced customer life cycle management facilities. Something we all refer to as call centers. Call center jobs are one of the most in-demand jobs these days.

Call centers are a critical component of the cost reduction strategies of organizations, which in turn help organizations to provide their goods and services at competitive prices to the customers.

Despite all efforts put in by organizations to handle all business areas, they have come to realize that by outsourcing their customer service operations, they are in a better position to build a brand name for their business. Over the years, business entities have come to realize that by either setting up call centers or by outsourcing their back office jobs to call centers that offer a portfolio of customer services leads to higher customer acquisition, satisfaction, retention, loyalty, and eventually positive purchase behaviors.

With a lot of mergers and acquisitions (M&A), consolidations and expansions occurring, call centers are the best way of dealing with the needs and requirements of an expanding business. To compete with others and capture a larger share of the market, business entities need to keep their customers happy. This is where call centers step in. As it is an age of research and development, call centers can take care of your back office services, customer support and technical support, whereas the rest of your organization can focus on strategic decisions, implementation models, expansion, research and development, and other core areas. This helps in cutting down on overheads like recruitment expenses and administrative costs too. This factor makes call centers as the catalysts for business transformation.

Another major benefit is the monetary saving factor. The investment in the form of fees for outsourcing to call centers is reasonable as compared to paying full-time staff.

The change in outlook towards managing call center-oriented services has made organizations become futurist in their approach, and they are willing to invest in new technologies and infrastructural facilities to offer 'better than the best' solutions.

It is estimated that every dollar of U.S. labor cost assigned overseas generates $1.12-$1.14 in excess thereby making outsourcing to third world countries a financially sound option for organizations.

Over the last decade or so, offshore outsourcing services have increased manifold due to a gamut of reasons—incredible cost savings, operational success, professional results, 24/7 well-designed services, technology advances and more. All these factors have made it possible to communicate complex information in real-time.

Outsourcing also helps organizations to make better use of their resources, time and money for enhancing the quality of their core functions. Another good reason for the expansion of call centers is that they allow organizations to focus on their internal staff and their development.

Spotlight Tip
With Web 2.0 and advanced technologies, call centers have become the vehicle of lead generation. They have become a corporate discipline in themselves.

1.3 Types—From Inbound to Blended

Call centers fall into various types based on their functions, areas of operation and the medium through which they communicate. Generally there are two main types—inbound and outbound. Another broad-level classification is that of domestic and international. Domestic call centers deal with customers within their own country. International call centers deal with customers on all points of the world compass. Over the years, as technologies advanced and customer demands increased, several other types developed based on various new factors like mobility, integration of applications, multi-channel services, etc. No matter what category a call center belongs to, its main purpose is that of helping organizations to streamline their operations.

Some organizations that handle a variety of calls, categorize call centers based upon the type of contact—a group for web chat, a group for inbound calls and so on and so forth.

The main types of call centers are explained in the following subsections:

1.3.1 Inbound—A Growing Part of the Global Economy

Inbound call centers make up a large and growing part of the world economy. Inbound call centers predominantly or exclusively field a large volume of incoming calls for various purposes like interactive voice response, catalog orders, customer service, order processing, help desk, website response, toll-free response, technical support, etc. They provide customer service by integrating a variety of technologies like Interactive Voice Response (IVR), Internet and telephones.

The performance of inbound CSRs is measured based on parameters like average call duration, average wait time, number of calls abandoned, etc.

Once a customer calls, there are various routing technologies, call management functions and call distribution methods needed to connect the customer call to an appropriate CSR. In case there is no CSR available immediately, the call is placed in a queue (a queue is the area that holds callers until the next agent is available). There are several scenarios that can occur after this stage: 1) The customer hangs up immediately after he/she is put on hold. 2) The customer holds on for some amount of time and then hangs up. 3) The customer holds on until he/she gets connected to a CSR and is provided with appropriate information or further transferred/handed off to another department/queue/agent. These scenarios mean a lot of factors that call centers need to monitor: 1) Average Time to Abandonment is defined as the average time that callers wait in queue before abandoning calls. 2) Queue Time also called as Delay is the time a caller spends in queue, waiting for an agent to become available. 3) Fast Clear Down means a caller who hangs up immediately when they hear a delay announcement. When all lines are in use, a delay announcement is played; it is a recorded message sent to callers while they are waiting in queue in order to let them know the approximate time they need to hold on before a CSR attends to them.

At the close of each call, CSRs are expected to key in codes for various types of post-call operations in terms of follow-up actions, data entry and the type of transaction.

These call centers also perform an important function of predicting customer behavior through account management and reporting capabilities. This function provides the inputs for their call-related decisions. Real-time management helps to make necessary adjustments in thresholds and staffing levels in response to current parameters such as call volume and queue conditions.

The main aim of inbound call centers is to increase sales and profit, increase the base of loyal customer advocates and minimize costs per sale. They provide 24/7 non-technical and technical support, and typically handle requests, queries and complaints in areas like account assistance, directory inquiry, sales, payment collection, billing and many more.

1.3.2 Outbound—Build Brand Loyalty

In outbound call centers, employees make the calls and these calls offer a medium for customized interactions that are driven by the customers.

The performance of outbound CSRs is measured in terms of productivity figures, conversion rates and sales quotas.

CSRs initiate a call to a customer mostly to sell a product or a service; their work is akin to salesmanship. These calls are either made through cold calling or warm calling approaches. Cold calling is the practice of making unsolicited calls to the potential customers. Warm calling is the practice of making calls to the customers who have had some contact with the representative's organization in the past or are a part of a list of names which has been qualified to receive calls. Dedicated professionals also called as marketing representatives (MR) who are trained for specific customer applications handle calls based on the customer's details and customized scripts.

Outbound call centers perform mainly sales-oriented operations like product promotion, lead generation, surveys, market research and intelligence. They also perform operations like appointment scheduling, verification services, account upgrades, credit management, database selling, etc. They also disseminate information regarding their organization's new products and services through subscription offers and telephone marketing.

The outreach programs carried out through outbound calls let organizations put a finger on the pulse of their customers, and that too in real-time. This one-to-one marketing option helps to convince the customers that they are of great value to organizations.

Follow-up on problems the customers are experiencing is another important function that outbound call centers perform.

1.3.3 Web-Enabled—Real-Time Interaction

Internet is the order of the day. Web-enabled call centers facilitate organizations to reach their clientele on any point of the world compass.

With web-enabled call centers, the customers can make a voice call to a call center online instead of calling on the telephone. They are not only used for communication and information propagation, but also used for carrying out business operations. They provide easy accessibility anytime, anywhere in the world. They offer the highest level of real-time interaction between the customers and CSRs. Other benefits include lower acquisition costs, smarter online customer care and higher lead conversion rates.

Web-enabled call centers require CSRs to be technically sound. Here calls are received from a link on a website. Typically, such websites have a "talk" button that connects the customers to a call center by scheduling a callback or through an Internet telephony connection. Microphones and speakers are needed for this type of a service delivery channel. In case microphones and speakers are not available, the appropriate voice encoding and decoding plug-in must be used.

Features like Call Through and Call Me make web-enabled call centers popular. Call Through is a feature where the customers have a simultaneous communication exchange with a CSR using Voice over Internet Protocol (VoIP) while they are still browsing an organization's website. Call Me also called click-to-call is a feature which converts website clicks into phone calls, text chats or VoIP. This feature provides an easy way for the website visitors to reach the call center team. It requires the website visitor to enter his/her phone number in order for CSRs to respond through callback.

There are several other convenient features like an instant E-Mail response, co-browsing, web callback, web pop and web chat that help CSRs to operate in real-time, right from obtaining caller information to providing support.

1.3.4 Telephone—Personalized Call Management

Telephone call centers offer personalized call management through advanced telephony and Internet technologies. Several organizations find it difficult to strike a balance between the workload and call load, so the best option for them is telephone call centers.

These call centers consist of professionals who are able to provide first-line service. In the case of complex calls, they can direct the call to appropriate organization personnel. They help in eliminating meaningless calls.

They also come in handy in various scenarios like when an organization's employees are on vacation or involved in some other projects.

1.3.5 CRM—Long-Term Relationships

Customer Relationship Management (CRM) call centers aim at long-term relationship building. Their entire focus is on customer interactions and they help organizations in identifying the most valuable customers. The customers communicate through a variety of options like Web chat, E-Mail, VoIP and many others.

The CRM solution integrates all forms of communication options through a centralized database. This database helps in the storage and productive usage of vast amounts of valuable customer data, organization sales and call history thereby reducing call durations, follow-up calls and costs. Call history helps CSRs to generate new leads and create additional sales.

CRM call centers also have user-friendly features and interactive reporting tools that aid the call center teams to generate accurate reports, which in turn help them in arriving at strategic decisions.

1.3.6 Virtual—Seamless Call Management

Virtual call centers go beyond the physical boundaries of the traditional brick and mortar model to incorporate geographically dispersed locations. They allow seamless call routing and management across an organization through a web of agents present in multiple locations.

In this environment, agents either work from the comfort of their homes or any other location. The customers calling a virtual call center may be under the impression that they are connecting to a physical call center, but in reality, their calls may have reached a stay-at-home mother, a telework center or any other remote location.

Organizations either utilize virtual call center agents themselves or hire services operated by third party organizations and they rent their setup through virtual ACD (VACD). An integrated skills-based routing technology is used to deliver calls to the most suitable virtual customer service representative.

Spotlight Tip
There are several benefits like lower employee turnover rates, flexible work timings, lower operational costs, and employment opportunities for people like disabled people or stay-at-home mothers.

Some virtual call centers require agents to work during weekends or evening hours, and even for seasonal business scenarios.

According to AMR Research (AMR Research is a research firm and is a part of Gartner), organizations using virtual call centers increase productivity by 15 percent and save an estimated one million dollars per 100 call center agents.

They also help in eliminating commuting cost, reducing pollution, etc. The flexibility of work location and timings attract a lot of people to this type of a call center.

1.3.7 Telemarketing—Direct in Approach

Telemarketing call centers provide the most direct way of finding qualified leads and tapping unexplored realms of potential customers. If operated properly in terms of personnel training, processes and technology, they prove to be successful in establishing a lifelong partnership with the customer base.

Marketing of products and services over the telephone is called telemarketing. The main aim of a telemarketing call center is promotion of products and services—it can be inbound or outbound sales. Apart from sales and marketing, a whole gamut of tasks is performed, right from appointment scheduling to lead qualification and from Business to Business (B2B) services to Business to Consumer (B2C) services.

They are a great way to follow-up on existing leads and generate new leads.

1.3.8 Blended—Effective Across Channels

The market for blended call centers is burgeoning. They have features of both inbound and outbound call centers; they take incoming calls and place outbound calls too. Blended call centers may well be the future of call centers as more and more organizations begin to offer all the services being demanded by the customers.

Large organizations have the investment muscle and management capabilities to have specialized CSRs dedicated for both inbound and outbound scenarios. In the case of smaller organizations, having two specialized groups is a costly affair. This is where call blending comes in handy. In call blending, organizations handle a mixture of calls by employing universal agents. In this scenario, CSRs are rotated between inbound and outbound call operations.

They also come into play when we talk of blending the various types of interaction channels, for example, a blended outbound call center is one that makes calls through a combination of phones, Fax and E-Mail.

Combining automatic call distribution for incoming calls with predictive dialing for outbound calls is the future. Blended call centers are becoming popular for their dynamic services and flexibility. They are more efficient than either inbound or outbound call centers as they have the capability to handle shortfalls and overflows in all scenarios of call management.

1.4 Applications—Sustain Organizational Competencies

Call center applications are about leveraging technology to define, develop and sustain organizational competencies in order to meet the workforce and customer needs. Call center applications create opportunities for value-added customer experiences.

Spotlight Tip
The types of services offered (customer acquisition, customer support or any other service) hugely influence the type of applications implemented.

Some of the main applications are discussed in the following points:

A. Billing

30 percent to 50 percent of call center calls are related to billing issues. Call centers in the billing domain handle all invoices/billing-related problems and requests, for example, customer queries regarding billing charges and interest rates. They handle all types of services, right from simple customer issues to reminder calls and from refunds to renewal or cancellation of subscription.

They interface with the accounts department to carry out the billing and collection functionalities successfully. Their main aim is to identify and correct billing failures at the source so that customer loyalty is not lost and operational costs are kept at the minimum.

B. Help Desk/Customer Support

Call centers that form a part of the customer service and support function (CSS) are typically referred to as a help desk. It is the first-line of support and offers a constant presence for the customers thereby reducing service disruptions and downtime.

Customer service is one of the prime functions of call centers. Organizations that sell products and services need to offer customer services in order to retain the customer base.

Apart from handling calls related to software and hardware troubleshooting, help desks also deal with aspects like tech support issues, product installation, compatibility problems and account setup issues. Customer support is an integral part of customer services.

C. Collections

Does someone owe you money for the product or service you offered? This is where collection agencies come into play. They are mainly responsible for collecting money or funds that are past due. Typical examples are that of insurance, medical debt, credit card collection, accounts receivables and mortgage payment. Third-party collection agencies often work on a commission basis; they receive a certain percentage of the funds that they manage to collect from delinquent accounts.

Call centers specializing in collection services operate on the basis of various factors like the age of the account, credit report, type and amount of debt, credit worthiness, etc.

They lessen the burden on organizations by handling debt collection activities and smoothing out the cash flow.

D. Technical Support

With the increasing use of technology in current times, technical support has become very critical. Technical support is about providing high-availability services according to varying needs of the callers.

For the customers, the quality of technical support provided is just as important as the quality of the product/service itself. Technical support is all about addressing issues, right from the most common issues to the most complex problems related to software, hardware and network. Most organizations provide technical support for the products they sell, either freely available or for a fee.

The customers of technology products and services need the services of technical experts all the time. There is a wide spectrum of expertise needed to handle the various areas of tech support, right from installation of hardware and software to maintenance and post implementation follow-up.

Most call centers these days follow the multi-tiered support model. There are various levels of technical support. This multi-tiered support model helps to better serve your business and customer base. The first level is for basic issues; it is also referred to as front-end support or first-line support. Level 2 is about handling in-depth troubleshooting. Level 3 denotes the highest level of support for handling complex problems within a call center. The last level is level 4, which is the highest escalation point and the support is provided by software and hardware vendors. Each of the levels is not only responsible for assisting the previous levels, but also developing solutions to new and unknown issues.

E. Sales

The main function is that of attracting and retaining the customers by positioning the sale from the buyer's perspective. Call centers handling the sales aspect of business need to improve the sales volume to meet the sales quotas. This is achieved based on a detailed study and research of market conditions and fluctuations, customer buying patterns, analysis of new markets, field reports about customer reactions, etc.

Product/service knowledge and sales skills are important to cater to the customer needs across channels. Sales call centers coordinate with several other departments like marketing, production and advertising to ensure sales stimulation and to uncover hidden revenue streams.

They utilize several methods like sales programs, surveys and direct marketing initiatives to reach out to new markets, to identify up-sell opportunities and to design ways of reinforcing successful sales behaviors.

Apart from the above services, there is a gamut of other applications like invoice payment, insurance marketing, claims reporting, inquiry services, appointment reminders, locator services, emergency notification and many more that call centers handle.

1.5 Outsourcing Options—Break Even

Outsourcing or sub-servicing is the process of entering into a contract with an outside organization/third party, and this outside organization/third party is responsible for handling tasks, operations and jobs passed on to it from the client. These are handled either on-site or off-site.

Organizations use call center outsourcing for either some or all of their services. The reason for the growing popularity of outsourcing is that more and more business entities have come to realize that the balancing factor for reducing overhead costs and increasing profits is *outsourcing*.

Organizations can follow any one or a combination of the following outsourcing routes:

A. Offshoring: The business processes or services are transferred overseas, to a distant organization.

B. Domestic: In domestic outsourcing, both the client and the service provider reside in the same country.

C. Virtual: Virtual call centers can be established anywhere. They facilitate off-site agents across multiple locations to operate as a single unit.

D. Nearshoring: Nearshoring is a derivative of the term offshoring. It is the shifting of work to nearby countries in the same or similar time zones. For example, some of the nearshoring locations for US organizations are Canada and Mexico. Other factors considered while nearshoring are physical proximity, cultural affinity, length of the project and language.

E. Captive Centers: These call centers serve the needs of their parent organization or group, for example, HSBC and GE.

A Word of Caution
Outsourcing is not a universal remedy to organizational problems. If organizations are facing internal problems, then outsourcing is not always the only solution, but reviewing and reinventing internal factors is required.

Over the past several years, the key areas of outsourcing that have developed are as follows:

A. Full Outsourcing
B. Web-based Outsourcing
C. Outsourcing of key transactions and unique processes
D. Offshore Outsourcing
E. Technology Services Outsourcing
F. Business Process Outsourcing (BPO)
G. Knowledge Process Outsourcing (KPO)
H. Medical Business Process Outsourcing (MBPO)
I. Seasonal Traffic
J. Apart from these areas, several other areas like Financial Reporting, Facilities Maintenance, Training, Claims Processing, Workflow Improvement, Marketing, Property Management, etc., are major players in the outsourcing space.

Here again, there are various options for delivering customer service. First, you can outsource to a third party, something like a service bureau. Second, an organization can outsource to a call center which is run by the organization itself—a core competency unit. The third option is a combination of these two.

1.6 The Outsourcing Decision—Various Dimensions

Outsourcing is not just a part of the business strategy, but it is also an integral component of the corporate culture. Organizations need to be sure that outsourcing fits in their culture and flows with their business. At the same time, organizations need to ensure that their outsourcing partners/ service providers are not rigid in their outlook rather their policies and practices need to move along with their client business needs.

Before arriving at a decision regarding outsourcing, there are several questions and factors that an organization needs to work out—are there any hidden costs involved, does the service provider show inclination in terms of business culture and seamless operation, and are there guarantees and continuous support available. All the financial, pricing and legal issues should be clearly stated in the contract and a 100 percent buy-in from the stakeholders involved is a must.

Outsourcing is about coexistence and mutual growth of the stakeholders involved in the process. Organizations need to understand their stakeholders' stand in regards to outsourcing. They should go ahead only if their stakeholders are willing to embrace this strategy.

The number of customers and the volume of calls is another factor that needs to be taken into consideration before arriving at a decision.

As with any major business purchase, organizations should request testimonials and references of both current and former clients of the outsourcing partner. Organizations need to cross-check the details of the services being delivered by the outsourcing provider in terms of quality control, accountability, scalability of services, best practices and customizable solutions by calling the references.

Organizations can seek professional opinion by talking to experts, business support organizations, professional groups and peers as they are in a position to provide firsthand information about various options and their impact.

Another equation that organizations need to balance is that of the complexity level of transactions and the customer value. A combination of low-value customers and less complex transactions is normally handled through the offshore outsourcing option. In the case of high-value customers and complex transactions, an in-house center is the best option.

The size of the project is a critical dimension that organizations need to study before finalizing the service provider. For a small project, one can contact freelancers. In the case of large, complex projects, an established service provider is the best option.

These factors help organizations in choosing the right vendor thereby ensuring service continuity.

1.6.1 Advantages—From Cost-Effectiveness to Core Competencies

The main advantages of outsourcing are discussed in the following points:

A. Organizations gain competitive advantage as all non-core functions are taken care of by the outsourcing partner. This allows organizations to concentrate on their core functions, which leads to an overall increase in efficiency.

B. Lower risk rates as the outsourcing partner/service provider is in a better position to manage and mitigate risks.

C. Organizations are able to start their operations/projects as soon as possible as the outsourcing partner/service provider has all the processes, practices, tools and resources in place. These capabilities of the outsourcing partner/service provider help in reducing the time-to-market factor.

D. Access to proven and cost-effective services results in quick deliverables, and eventually loyal customers.

E. Easy access to operational expertise, skills and a wider knowledge base, which otherwise, in the in-house scenario will take a long time to build and nurture.

F. In order to cater to various business processes and transactions, organizations need to invest in new tools and technologies, infrastructure and business models. At times, such investment may not generate the break even profit. In such cases, organizations consider the option of outsourcing the work to specialized personnel or third-party firms.

G. Wages in developing countries are lower than advanced nations resulting in something called as "Labor Arbitrage". Outsourcing to developing countries helps in reducing labor costs, which in turn can be used in enhancing the quality of the in-house staff.

Learning Organizations—Competitive Advantage

2

C for continuous learning, C for call times down and call volumes up, C for round-the-clock customer service, and C for call centers as learning organizations. We have transitioned from the Industrial Age to the Era of Knowledge Workers, and call centers are an integral part of this transition. Call centers are *hubs of transformation* in themselves as they provide a dashboard of tools and technologies, which are used to convert vast amounts of information into knowledge—Value Addition to your organization as well as your customers. Learning and knowledge acquisition are the keystone of each and every call center. This very drive for learning is the reason for the leads that eventually get translated into sales.

While numbers, metrics and statistics play an important role in call centers, but what really determines the true value of call centers—the answer is the quality and efficiency of their knowledge workers. This chapter discusses the various aspects needed to convert the information at your fingertips into knowledge that helps your call center to deal with complex customer problems, account-related questions, sales and sales support, information inquiries and product support requests.

Differentiation is drawn from the "how" versus the "what" is sold. Call centers feed on their daily *collective* corporate learnings to leverage this differentiation and to deal with the dynamics of the knowledge economy.

2.1 First Impressions Count—Happy, Loyal Customers

All customers are unique—they all have their own individual tastes, perceptions and preferences. Retaining the customers is of utmost importance and one of the ways of doing so is by having a call center. Research findings indicate that organizations can boost their profits by almost 100 percent by retaining just 5 percent of their customers. Neither promotional campaigns nor marketing strategies get the customers to call in the first place. It is the service that the customers receive motivates them to come back again and again.

Call center customer contact cycles are not lengthy ones; hence you have to create an interest in the customer's mind in the first twenty seconds in order to generate long-term customer equity. In the case of inbound services, 80 percent of the calls need to be answered in 20 seconds; this is the business standard. Qualities like cognitive skills, voice clarity, neutral accent, fluency and grammar play an important role here.

The term *First Call Resolution* (*FCR*) is not just a mere term, but it is the key factor in improving customer satisfaction; it is the measure that matters the most. FCR=Customer's request or problem is resolved in one call. For every 1 percent improvement in FCR, you get a 1 percent improvement in customer satisfaction, and this helps in doing away with unnecessary call backs. Before moving on to any sort of sales transactions, CSRs must be successful in meeting customer needs. Improving FCR is also important in reducing employee stress level and turnover rate. It is always important to measure FCR based on customer feedback as it gives a clear picture of where a call center stands. People and processes thrive when they learn how to utilize customer feedback. This goes to show how important the customer is!

It is important to remember that most customers put customer service ahead of price in their purchasing decision. What starts as a simple call can turn out to be a lifelong relationship, which facilitates repeat business. As the saying goes, you never get a second chance to make a first impression—this holds good for the call center scenario too. The same customer may call several times, but it is rare for the same CSR to handle these multiple requests. Thus, it is essential to handle calls professionally and effectively the first time itself, and minimize after-call work. After-call work is also called post-call processing or wrap-up; it is the work that immediately follows an inbound transaction. When it comes to operating a call center, it is imperative that the customers come back to you again and again. This is possible only when you make that 'great first long-lasting impression' on them.

A little extra effort in making callers feel that you are happy to have them onboard as customers will go a long way for your business. Right from the initial contact interaction with the customers to the follow-up calls, CSRs need to extend courteous service by providing accurate information and demonstrating up-to-date product and service knowledge.

Front-line fundamentals include essential aspects like first-class phone etiquettes and skills, apt voice dynamics, welcome words and power phrases. Match your pace of talking to that of the customers so that a comfort level is established between both the parties. It is imperative to use words that project a personable tone. At the same time, it is essential to give verbal cues to the customers that you are listening to them with laser-sharp attention. Examples of verbal cues are "Yes, go on", "Please tell me more", "I understand what you must be going through", etc. These tips facilitate a healthy knowledge exchange.

Spotlight Tip
Treat each call as if it were the first call of the day. As call center interaction is vocal in nature, it is necessary that you as a CSR smile when appropriate. Your smile transmits positive vibes to the customer as it comes across in your voice. Rephrase negative statements into positive ones, for example, saying: "Thank you for being so patient" is much more positive than "I am sorry you had to wait so long".

Personalizing each and every call is one major component needed in building a great first impression. Using phrases like "Thank you for using our product." or "Is there anything else I can help you with?" or "Have a nice day!" ensure a great rapport between the customers and CSRs.

A CSR's voice should not only be courteous and polite, but must be impregnated with sincerity and concern too. CSRs need to ensure that the customers feel their empathy through the use of appropriate phrases like "sorry for the inconvenience caused", "we will definitely work out an effective solution", etc. Show support and not sympathy.

2.1.1 Important Pointers—Stand Out in the Crowd

Here are important pointers to ensure that the customers remain loyal to the products and services, and more importantly remain loyal to the brand itself:

A. Identify yourself at the beginning of the call. In the case of outbound calls, share your name as well as the details of the organization you are representing. Calls with a name sound professional, whereas unidentified calls sound suspicious and unsolicited in nature.

B. No matter how demanding the customers are, open and end the communication cycle with kind greetings.

C. Know your product and service offerings well. In-depth knowledge of the products and services along with the knowledge of competition help you to convince the customers that your organization is the best by giving them a vigilant comparative analysis.

D. The customer is always right. Do not blame or criticize the customer's claims, instead listen attentively, think twice before speaking and then offer help.

E. Express your caring attitude with a calm voice. Ask apt questions to get to the bottom of the problem/request. In the case of a sales deal, PID/PIQ qualifiers play an important role. They are questions that assist CSRs to solicit critical inputs from a prospect, which are then used to present the right information to a prospect and close a sale.

F. Ensure that you continue using phrases like *thank you, please give me a moment*, etc., to reassure the customers that they and their needs are precious to the organization.

G. Get involved in the process of customer service by asking close-ended questions. A close-ended question is answered as a simple "yes" or "no", or as a single-word answer or a short response; these straightforward answers help in closing a sale. This involvement helps to reduce the call time. Keep track of information already collected in order to increase the customer network.

H. Never retaliate or answer back. Focus on the problem and not on the irate behavior of the customers. The only way to pacify agitated callers is by applying facts and logic to arrive at a positive outcome.

I. In the case of making calls to a customer, ensure that you call as per the customer's convenience. Giving priority to the customer's callback time requirements helps to develop long-term relationships. CSRs need to be trained to use outbound calling to their organization's advantage; outbound calling is a strong retention tool.

Each and every customer deserves equal, personalized attention and flexibility. Each customer call is just as crucial as the other calls.

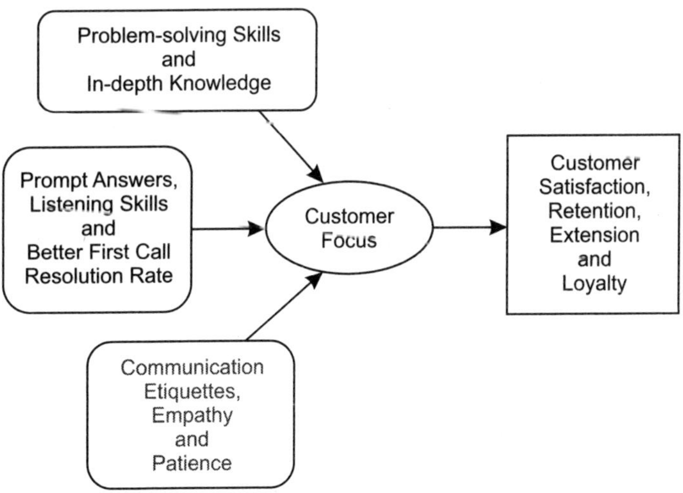

Figure 2.1: The Customer Focus Skills

CSRs need to "converse with the callers" rather than "talk to the callers". This live support environment, if used properly, will surely help your call center to stand out in the crowd.

2.2 Constant Training—A Forward-Looking Attitude

There is a common misconception people hold about call center jobs—people think that working in a call center is easy because it is just about answering phone calls. This is absolutely incorrect and baseless. Call centers require soft skills, time management abilities and multi-tasking. CSRs have to put up with extreme pressures. This is where comprehensive and regular training comes handy. Training is seen as a potential method to reduce turnover rates. Recent surveys show that increased training leads to a decrease in employee turnover.

The process of training the hired personnel is perhaps more important than the actual hiring process itself. The main aim of training is that each and every customer who comes in contact with CSRs ends up satisfied with the solution offerings.

The difference between success and failure is the quality of training imparted. Constant training and skills-upgrade programs are needed to keep CSRs in tune with the transactional load and service scalability. Branding is much more than logos, jingles and fancy taglines. CSRs are the real brand ambassadors for an organization; hence careful strategy, planning and individual needs analysis are needed to design training workshops and programs. They are a way of projecting a desirable organizational image; hence you will find smiling CSRs featured on billboards and print advertisements. They are the key resources who resolve customer complaints and fulfill customer requests. Call centers are essentially a services-driven sector. Customer care services are intangible in nature and that is why the customers determine the quality of customer care services provided based on the type of treatment they receive from the front-line staff.

The nature of training depends on the type of CSRs that need to be trained—whether inbound or outbound customer service representatives. Inbound customer services include responding to customer requests, resolving customer complaints or IVR, whereas in outbound customer services, CSRs call the key accounts directly and offer services like telemarketing, debt collection, appointment scheduling or surveys.

Training programs, workshops and role play exercises are like a safe-simulated environment to give enough of practice before CSRs actually start working in the real world. They instill the habit of valuing those skills that improve their ability to connect with the customers.

Customized training is necessary to bring about a results-oriented attitude within the employees. Training is not about instructions or a material-based session, but about looking at the future and generating long-term value from customer interactions. For the customers, the person on the other end of the line is the organization itself. Therefore, it is important for CSRs to be well-trained.

Some call centers are web-driven where customer queries and requests are resolved through live chat or e-mail. In this case, training is needed to instill Netiquettes in CSRs. Netiquette stands for Internet Etiquette; a set of rules for behaving properly in the online world. Today, not only organizations but also households have computers. The customers have also become net-savvy; hence CSRs need to transform themselves from mere "smile and dial" workers to "pitch and place" advocates of their organization. This transformation definitely encourages the customers to e-mail or employ any other form of net-driven communication to ask for more information about products and services. CSRs need to keep training themselves constantly, keep themselves abreast of latest technological advancements and update their knowledge of their organization's latest product and service offerings.

Soft skills like better image management, good listening, voice culture, empathy and a friendly approach need to be a part of the training curriculum and practical exercises. Cognitive skills must be developed for handling complex customer requests and delivering high-level services. Skills specific to the customer culture need to be imparted; these skills are needed so as to avoid culture-specific problems. For example, US-based callers expect that CSRs handle their calls with both empathy and prudence; hence training imparted should be in sync with the caller culture.

In current times, call center customer care is becoming more of a social networking scenario than just a technical resolution. It is about social networking going into business. Training should take care of such scenarios too.

In case your call center deals with customers across the globe, essentially customers who are non-English speaking, then you need to ensure that you recruit personnel who have the required level of proficiency in the preferred language of the customers, and this requirement needs to be coupled with continual multilingual skills development sessions. CSRs that are multilingual help to increase the number and type of customers; they help to acquire new foreign customers.

Generally, call centers conduct language training sessions during the induction period. These sessions are a huge benefit as they help the employees to improve their speaking skills.

From these dimensions, we can conclude that training in the following areas is necessary:

A. Build better customer relationships.

B. Handle call volume.

C. Deal with irate customers in a courteous manner.

D. Gain knowledge of the products and services.

E. Project a positive image of the organization.

F. Generate value addition through up-selling and cross-selling. Up-selling is a sales strategy whereby CSRs convince their customers to increase the value of their orders in terms of add-ons, upgrades or more expensive products/services. Cross-selling is a sales technique in which CSRs push new products/services to current customers based on their past purchases. This technique decreases the likelihood of the customers defecting to competitors. The most effective way of capitalizing on these techniques is to design a sales strategy outside-in; successful selling starts by selecting the right segment of customers and then working backward by developing the apt value proposition unique to the segment.

G. Develop and review personal mission statements from time to time to bring them in sync with organizational goals.

H. Listening comprehension is a very important skill that all CSRs should possess. Whether it is the inbound or outbound scenario, a CSR must not forget to listen in between the lines for the underlying tone, key words and context anchors, attitudes and emotions, and new opportunities. Neither interrupt callers nor pre-empt what they are going to say. Successful listening comprehension results in the learning of new information and insights. More understanding leads to more learning, and more learning leads to more knowledge.

Illustration 2.1: Listening Comprehension is Very Important

All these aspects need to have a central place in the training agenda so that the call center employees can deal with the multi-channel communication interfaces and aid in reducing a high customer churn rate. It is always better to train CSRs in such a way that they are cross-trained to handle a variety of transactions across communication channels and are able to fit into the world of virtualization.

A Word of Caution
Training needs to have both a short-term focus and a long-term view. Merely focusing on improved customer service is not enough. Trainees need to be taught how to use information to handle customer interaction and how to use customer interaction data to establish market insights and fine-tune processes.

Training revamps need to occur on a regular basis in order to make the skills acquired by CSRs, their excellence. Call centers need to ensure that employee communities of practices are created and trained in order to disseminate and capitalize on insights, lessons learned and observations captured during the workflow cycle.

2.3 Accent Neutralization—Use the Customer's Language

In this communication-based corporate space, no one likes to endlessly repeat themselves while interacting, especially because of a heavy, choppy accent. Certain groups of speakers of English are known to speak much faster than people in the West, which results in speed mismatch and communication barriers. Accent neutralization in terms of accent modification, word stress, speech improvement, syllable stress, speaking rate and voice enhancement is the answer to avoiding communication hurdles and doing away with regional biases. In short, accent neutralization is the process of developing an accent which is not influenced by one's regional background or native language. To speed up this process, you can always refer to my book on the importance of English in today's world of globalization, *English Language: The Gateway to Global Growth*.

Accent neutralization is highly important in call centers as business is conducted in *real-time* and on a world-wide scale. It helps to build and improve the image of call centers. A neutral accent is important as it is understood globally; it is about deprecating regional biases by changing rhythm, speech patterns and intonation to suit the customers. There is no second chance—whatever needs to be achieved should to be achieved in the first call itself. The main purpose of accent neutralization is speaking a language in such a way which is understood by the native speakers as well as people who use it as their official/ second language.

The main reason for the popularity of accent neutralization is the ever-increasing demand of outsourcing opportunities. Merely having a great grasp of the English language is not enough. As the customer's primary contact, CSRs need to both understand the customer's message correctly and respond in the apt accent accordingly. They need to project a good social and corporate image of their organization to the outside world, and this can be done by using the customer's language.

The ideal speaking rate is between one hundred forty and one hundred sixty words per minute. The best way to achieve this rate is by timing yourself while reading newspaper articles. Each day read for about 10 minutes and continue with this routine until you have reached the desired rate, and then you will be able to perform well in the monitored and time-sensitive environment of a call center.

A Word of Caution
Accent neutralization does not mean accent elimination or cultural decay. It is a process of facilitating intelligible communicative exchange between global speakers.

Research shows that people who can communicate well and be easily understood perform well. There are several ways of overcoming a heavy accent and becoming a great communicator:

A. If English is your second language, then a professional accent neutralization class is a good option for non-native speakers to acquire the appropriate intonation patterns and native-level pronunciation. By using the correct pitch and stress, CSRs are able to improve their intonation, and eventually be understood by western callers.

B. By observing and listening to native speakers such as TV reporters, hosts, etc., CSRs will be able to control their accent.

C. Master the sound specifics in terms of the vowels and consonants. Factors like understanding the difference between sounds, whether long or short, and getting the length of the vowel/consonant right, make a big difference in the communication flow.

D. Call center employees need to familiarize themselves with the sounds of the target language, which most of the times is English. Since call centers operate in a multi-cultural economy, the knowledge of the International Phonetic Alphabet (IPA) helps CSRs to differentiate between pairs of sounds, for example, *day and they*. IPA helps them to understand customer inputs flawlessly and operate effectively on a cross-cultural platform.

E. Easy to use monikers also ease the process.

In summary, accent neutralization creates the following benefits:

A. Enhanced job prospects and growth opportunities.

B. Easy movement within the western culture.

C. Global audience; hence global perspective.

D. Flexibility of switching from an American client to a British one, and vice versa.

E. More confidence, both personally and professionally.

F. Improved telephone skills, negotiation skills and social skills.

G. An edge over the others.

At the superficial level, accent neutralization may seem to be about voice-related aspects. But in reality, it is about managing knowledge, experiences and relationships from each and every customer's perspective. Accent neutralization leads to the assimilation of a new culture, and not its imitation.

2.4 Knowledge Workers—Real-Time Results

Call center employees are knowledge workers transcending all hierarchical barriers in order to build a knowledge-driven performance and customer experience culture. Their services are value-added services evolving and reshaping the call center world constantly.

Their work is not limited to routine data collection and solving technical problems, but also entails processing, analyzing, converting, creating and applying new knowledge. Working in a call center setup is about creating, capturing and co-sharing knowledge reserves to participate in productive work, establish new strategies, create new solutions, widen the talent pipeline, and generate ideas for new products and services. According to International Data Corporation (IDC is a market research and analysis firm), Fortune 500 organizations lose at least $31.5 billion a year as they fail to adequately share knowledge (Babcock, 2004). Thus, it is extremely crucial to absorb and incorporate knowledge and experiences within an organization. This transfer of knowledge is needed to learn from the past lessons, to get access to solutions to already handled problems, to build trust for new knowledge value, and eventually to build and expand organizations.

Apart from being hardworking and willing to learn, call center employees need to be driven by knowledge. The first 20 seconds of a call is all you get to sell your ideas to the customers. As a CSR, merely listening to the customers is not enough; you also need to gather information about their needs and preferences. Insights into the customers' psyche help CSRs to tailor their responses and make decisions on the fly.

One very important way of building both the knowledge base and customer base is taking notes of whatever facts and figures the customers share. These notes are a great input for the customer feedback loop, both during the call and after the call, and also while performing market surveys and product/service promotion campaigns. These notes also help organizations to avoid the trap of factual errors as they have everything in black and white. Up-to-date knowledge and authentic facts help to create accurate, revenue-generating and engaging communication experiences.

Customer profiling, and document retrieval and archival systems also enhance the knowledge levels of CSRs. Customer profiling helps in identifying key customer characteristics and segments where you can find more high-value customers. A document retrieval and archival system is an electronic and interactive database that keeps track of a vast amount of digital documents, provides universal access to customer communications and improves response handling time.

A Word of Caution
If you fail to look at the BIG picture, then the bottom line is bound to suffer. Call centers are not just about managing the interaction cycle, but are also about delivering results by providing credible and authentic knowledge.

The duty of front-line leaders and supervisors is not just confined to using the screen monitoring feature of remotely keeping a watch on the activity on CSRs' computer terminals; it is much more than that. Front-line leaders and supervisors need to instill the knowledge of corporate values in CSRs so that they maintain loyalty towards the overall corporate framework and agenda. Leaders, managers and supervisors also need to follow the common practice of MBWA—Management By Walking Around. MBWA is a common call center practice where managers and supervisors adopt an open door policy by physically visiting their CSRs and having face-to-face contact with them in order to motivate them, address their work-related issues, listen to their suggestions and recognize their contributions. MBWA is about establishing a stable, equitable corporate culture.

To someone on the outside, call center jobs may appear as highly routine jobs, but in reality, call center employees equate to a corporate culture of constant learning and knowledge sharing.

Spotlight Tip
Effective front-line leadership motivates CSRs to be driven by a combination of knowledge and passion. Highly motivated CSRs are more engaged in their jobs.

Knowledge workers in a call center are the ones who have the power to transform a simple office setup to a multi-channel, multi-level, multi-modal, multi-dimensional and multi-shore outsourcing unit by collaborating through their unique "know-how". Therefore, a call center needs to generate opportunities for employees to collaborate with leading-edge talent, both within and outside their organization. This environment enables them to successfully resolve progressively more difficult challenges.

On the one hand, organizations provide a lucrative learning environment to call center employees, whereas on the other hand, these employees facilitate the application of *collective* intelligence to personalize and optimize each customer call.

2.4.1 Knowledge Worker Management—Superior Service

The focus of business success has shifted from manufacturing efficiency to knowledge management. With constant changes that affect the business landscape, managers of organizations have come to realize that knowledge in the form of various sources of information needs to be collected, analyzed and acted upon.

"Hard data" is one part of the equation, but what completes the knowledge management equation is the human source of knowledge in the form of employee's perceptions, experiences, cognitive patterns and insights. For keeping this equation balanced, personnel need to be motivated and trained to transform this knowledge into value by using it not only for analyzing the past, but also for accommodating the future challenges and opportunities.

The shift from manufacturing efficiency to knowledge-driven services has resulted in the corporate focus shifting from managing technology to managing knowledge. In order to act as an efficient link between Customer Experience Management (CEM) and Knowledge Management (KM), there are four most important new-age resources that a call center needs to concentrate on. These resources provide a 360 degree view of the customers and bring about knowledge management synergy:

A. Knowledge Base

B. Employees

C. Technology

D. Customers

These resources are the answers to knowledge generation, adaptation, dissemination and utilization.

Technology provides the right knowledge to the right employees, who in turn use this knowledge to provide the right services to the customers. Call centers should have technologies that make their CSRs data-aware representatives, and this is possible by integrating traditional call center metrics with modern setups like Customer Experience Management (CEM) and Customer Relationship Management (CRM). These integrated systems provide real-time alerts based on threshold values, which CSRs utilize to make informed decisions.

After-call Work (ACW) is an important post-call process, which enables agents to gather customer intelligence and knowledge of call-related aspects. This process provides inputs for formulating a knowledge-based plan of action to fill the performance gaps.

Connecting with the customers is of utmost importance as your customer base is your most reliable source of firsthand knowledge about the performance of your products and services. Their inputs help in improving and evolving a call center. This knowledge discovery and generation helps in decisions related to customer identification, customer behavior prediction and customer retention.

A call center Knowledge Base is a must have as it is the core storage point for collecting data about customer interactions and transactions, and maintaining historical information too. It must house only information that is relevant and innovative in nature. The base must be intuitive so information can be easily found, and it must allow for real-time inputs and real-time updates too. Again, such a base helps to measure customer retention, customer loyalty and the revenue potential through real-time business analytics. It also helps to operationalize innovation by converting knowledge into revenue growth. With the increased complexity in customer handling, it is necessary to handle data and statistics related to this aspect. Something we refer to as data mining; extraction of knowledge from the knowledge base for predicting trends and patterns.

Two main skills that need to be instilled in employees to transform them into knowledge workers are skills of reflection and skills of inquiry. Skills of reflection deal with our thinking patterns and mental models. They are about slowing down our thinking and reflecting on how it affects our behavior, decisions and actions. Skills of reflection help employees to avoid making baseless conclusions and generalizations, and rationalize their beliefs to display the most apt behavior and responses. Skills of inquiry deal with applying the skills of reflection in actual situations where employees work in unison by sharing all data, information and knowledge. Co-sharing of knowledge enables employees to act in a *transparent* fashion, to build and achieve common interests, and to arrive at intelligent conclusions based on each others' points of view.

Call centers need to provide adequate opportunities for creating diversity of ideas and developing a laser-sharp focus on long-term goals so that employees can instill confidence in the customers and make them feel safe in their transactions.

A culture that develops the risk-taking attitude of employees helps to bring together the knowledge bits and integrate disciplines to complete the business puzzle—customer selection, customer acquisition, customer retention and customer extension. So stop thinking calls and start thinking customer knowledge processing and sharing!

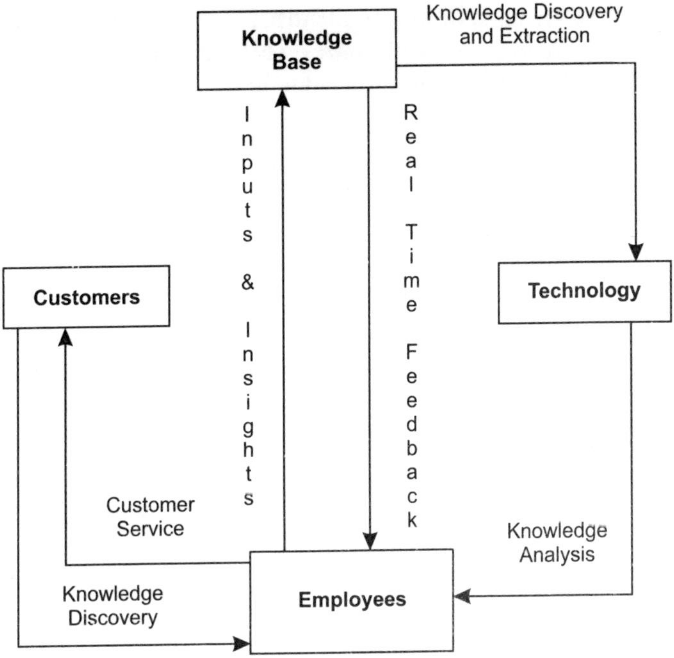

Figure 2.2: The Knowledge Management Cycle

2.4.2 Knowledge-Driven—Knowledge Culture Essentials

The knowledge culture essentials are aspects that help CSRs to reinforce the call center culture of knowledge sharing. The following is a checklist of these essentials:

A. Each and every novel customer problem needs a lot of patience, experimentation and tolerance. A true knowledge worker is one who handles this level of uncertainty with open-mindedness and courage; one who discovers the solution by 'thinking outside the box'.

B. High personal motivation levels in CSRs indicate that they are self-motivated to collect and convert data, information and knowledge into tacit wisdom, and finally into explicit actions. They have a strong belief in the value of knowledge sharing and adding value to their organization through it.

C. CSRs need to be able to identify patterns in the knowledge they synthesize and share. This quality helps them in identifying critical knowledge bits.

D. CSRs prove to be great knowledge workers when they show good networking abilities. They are not insular to new sources of knowledge; they believe in pushing their boundaries to increase the shareability factor. They value mutual interaction and collaboration, both through formal and informal ways.

E. Risk-taking is a must for any true knowledge worker to perform. Taking calculated risks to arrive at lucrative decisions is what a true knowledge worker does.

F. They are constantly developing cutting-edge skills. They are constantly in search of opportunities that provide them with challenges, which help them to test and refine their skills.

G. They exhibit the need to have the ability to link their knowledge reserves to the organizational goals and performance.

H. Honesty and trust are two integral traits that CSRs need to exhibit in all the processes related to knowledge management—acquisition, utilization, collaboration and generation.

A Word of Caution

Call centers that stunt the growth and freedom of their employees, limit their own growth. Call centers need to institute processes that create a liberal learning network, only then they can truly succeed as a knowledge-driven organization.

Accommodative leadership is crucial to nurture the above elements. For encouraging knowledge workers and promoting a knowledge-driven, customer-oriented experience paradigm, a comprehensive corporate learning strategy should be in place.

Human Factors—They are What Make a Call Center

3

Call centers operate in a services-driven economy. Today's competitive landscape is all about tapping into the right data and information to provide error-free services. Do you want to increase your call center sales figures? For this to happen, people need to be mentored, trained and retained as they symbolize the nerve center of call centers.

Here we discuss about how to develop various competencies—linguistic, interactive, etc. Leadership is very critical to the success of a call center. Front-line managers need to have the human skills to bring out the best in their teams.

Setting up a call center is not an end in itself. You need qualified, highly motivated and well-trained people to run the show. Recognizing and appreciating good work is the key to retaining people. This chapter discusses all this and more to help your call center employees to interpret, integrate and internalize the rapid flow of information. It deals with topics related to human resource management in call centers. The coaching challenges and solutions are discussed too.

3.1 Staffing Plan—The Recipe for the Right Team

A workable staffing plan requires accurate forecasting methods and statistics regarding the productivity of the current workforce in order to predict accurate workload, to identify any gap between projected supply and future demand and to design strategies to bridge the gaps. Quantitative forecasting is needed to plan for the staffing needs. Quantitative forecasting includes techniques like Time Series and Explanatory Models. These are apt for forecasting future events based on historical patterns, factual numbers and previous experiences. Another aspect to design a perfect plan is to study the statistics for your call center to determine your needs during the busiest periods. In case historical data is not available, call centers employ Qualitative forecasting methods; methods like educated guess, management intuition, market research, historical analogy and more scientific techniques like the Delphi technique where forecasts are made through group consensus by soliciting expert responses to questionnaires in two or more rounds.

An organization needs to determine the manpower needs of the business before developing the staffing plan as 60 to 65 percent of a call center's total costs are manpower-related expenses. As call centers operate on tight margins, having a foolproof plan results in better identification and utilization of human and technical resources. This goes a long way in ensuring that performance issues do not get swept under the carpet, and the difference between demand and supply factors is greatly minimized. Supply refers to the number of completed calls a call center expects to achieve at 100 percent productivity rate. Demand refers to the number of employees needed to achieve this objective.

The staff is the backbone of a call center and to keep their initial gusto intact, a well-rounded plan needs to be in place. Finding the right mix of various personalities in your team is a must and to do this you can refer to my record-setting book on self-directed work teams, *Organizational Democracy: Collaborative Team Culture: Key to Corporate Growth*.

Developing the staffing plan can be a time-consuming and challenging task. It is wise to bring in a call center consultant or an analyst so that all financial costs, constraints, resource availability and operational performance factors are taken care of. At the outset, the call center vision and main objectives need to be outlined and then estimates of the timing of work activities and their dependencies need to be made in order to decide on the type and number of employees needed—whether On-site, Remote or Work-at-Home agents. Remote or Work-at-Home agents are professionals who perform call center work without physically being present on the call center premises.

> **A Word of Caution**
>
> Treat the employees as the voice of the organization, not as a mere mouth piece. This approach helps to bring about overall integration through the staffing plan.

The plan should also contain details of how your workforce is to be mobilized depending on the type of staffing your organization employs—outsourcing, in-house, telecommuting or third party. This plan needs to also deal with the *Base Staff* component. Base Staff is also called Seated Agents; the minimum number of agents required to cover the base contact volume.

Workforce management (WFM) is an integral component of the staffing plan as it helps to strike a balance between organizational goals and human factors. The main aim of WFM is to balance the work volume with the resources needed to complete that work in order to avoid overstaffing or understaffing issues. Managing agents in relation to work schedules and workload is an intricate task.

Developing business objectives, delivery channels, sensible work schedules, service levels, skills inventory, gap analysis, recruitment plan, training sessions and retention strategies are all a part of a complete staffing plan.

Call center shrinkage refers to the time for which CSRs are paid but during which they are not available to take calls, for example, time lost in lunch, vacation, sickness, etc. Shrinkage considerations are often calculated as a percentage figure. To arrive at a realistic figure and to be able to meet the required service level, call centers need to take into account factors like actual availability of staff, schedule adherence and exception reporting while designing the staffing plan.

Scheduling software is needed to handle time management and determine the optimal number of staff required to manage the operations. There are several call center staffing tools to determine how many full-time agents are required. Popular computation tools like Erlang tools help to calculate the number of agents needed to handle the workload. The Erlang is a unit of traffic density/load in a telecommunications system. Erlang measurements and statistical tables (Erlang B, Extended Erlang B and Erlang C) help call centers to understand their traffic patterns, to calculate the staffing level, and to estimate the number of trunk lines required in a network or between a telephone system and a central location. A trunk line is a telephone circuit linking two switching systems.

Computerized shift planner software is a big time-saver as it provides easy-to-use templates for planning shift schedules and also ensures that everyone reports to work (no one misses a shift) through automatic e-mail alerts.

The staffing plan must also cater to a comprehensive on-boarding process so as to ensure that the new entrants comfortably plug into the corporate setting, connect to their teams, relate to the unwritten rules, accommodate themselves, and get engaged fully to provide round-the-clock customer services.

The big picture of your call center should not be overlooked. The long-term aspect of hiring, firing, retraining and retaining staff is important and needs to be given serious thought in line with several parameters like markets trends, call volume forecasts, future products and services, etc. Several versions of the plan may need to be created to map to several scenarios, right from the best case scenario to the most pessimistic scenario. Creating these versions is a herculean job, and you can combine the services and expertise of a consultant with the statistics and forecasts of modeling tools to ease the process.

Table 3.1: Essential Elements of the Staffing Plan

Elements	Functions
Statistics and Forecasting Methods	Predict accurate workload and staffing needs.
Workforce Management	Balances the work volume with the resources needed to complete that work.
On-boarding Process	Ensures that the new entrants comfortably plug into the corporate culture.
Services of a Consultant	Takes care of the financial costs, resource availability, constraints and operational performance factors.
Scheduling Software	Handles time management and determines the optimal number of staff required to manage the operations.

The quality of your staffing plan says more about your organizational culture than you think.

3.2 Recruiting and Hiring—Fair Practices

The recruitment plan is developed using findings from the gap analysis component. The process of recruiting and hiring the right personnel is a challenging task for the Human Resources department. Recruiting, screening and hiring involves defining an accurate job description and performance standards, identifying job-specific skills, matching the description and the skills through various sources of recruitment, and finally making the selection and extending the job offer. All these processes need to be executed in line with the organizational practices and legal considerations; no discrimination of any kind should be entertained. These processes ensure that standard and fair recruiting and hiring practices are followed, which in turn project an organization's image as fair and equitable.

3.2.1 Success Factors—Follow Them and See the Difference

Various factors determine the success rate of the recruiting, screening and hiring processes:

A. What kind of opportunities/portals/job fairs do you have access to? Networking plays a critical role in hiring top-notch people for a call center. The right kind of networking in terms of résumé services, print advertisements, placement portals, internal recommendations, advertising options and job fairs is essential for a high success rate.

B. The number of new-hires is a key input to the recruiting and hiring processes. This forecast is calculated based on factors like the size and type of a call center and seasonal workload. In scenarios like seasonal help where a large number of employees need to be recruited fast, recruitment software is used to speed up the recruiting process and cut down on time and money. The main advantage of such software is that it lets HR personnel to get straight to the qualified candidates and eliminates the need to invest in hiring the services of a recruitment consultancy.

C. There are several sources used to develop a pool of potential candidates like the referral system, current employees, job agencies, campus placements, interns, temporary staff and competitors. Call centers need to identify appropriate sources in order to design and execute source-specific recruitment and selection strategies successfully. Based on the job type and role, call centers decide on the type of hiring—internal or external. For example, in the case of supervisory and managerial positions, call centers prefer internal hiring. In the case of technical positions, call centers opt for external hiring so that they get the depth and breadth of industry exposure.

D. Screening methods are equally crucial, right from interviews to application forms and résumés and from various types of tests (aptitude, personality) to references. No matter what medium is used to test the candidate's knowledge, employers need to make sure that they include a good mix of structured and non-structured questions to be able to gauge the applicant's ability to do the job. The traditional interview questions are straightforward questions, for example, why did you choose this career or what are your long-term and short-term goals? Behavior-based questions are an important set of questions in discovering how candidates handled employment-specific situations in their past jobs, for example, how did you handle a difficult situation with a supervisor? Information collected during screening is useful in the final stage of the selection process.

E. To capitalize on the above sources and services, call centers need to perform thorough analysis in terms of investment in these sources and services, and the payoff from the same. Another crucial facet in striking a balance is that of the payback period too.

F. The amount of money allotted for employee referral schemes should be justified in terms of quality personnel recruited.

G. The amount of time the recruiting specialists, screening and hiring managers, and related HR personnel expend in scheduling and conducting interviews, screening résumés, short-listing candidates and doing follow-up needs to be estimated accurately. This factor is important in ensuring that the process is cost-effective, and at the same time, is also contributing to the productivity of a call center.

H. The location of a call center plays an important part in creating a potential labor pool. The right location is one where the educational level of a potential labor pool is high, language skills are present and the attitude of people towards the concerned call center is favorable.

I. Other costs that a call center may incur are the amount of money spent on accommodation, training, temporary housing, relocation, and scheduling factors like the number of temporary staff or part-time staff, etc., for new hires.

Spotlight Tip
Whether internal or external hiring—the main aim of call centers is in making certain the right candidate fills the right job post and the new hires are assimilated into the organizational culture.

Organizations need to constantly track their strategies for all the methods of recruitment and selection that they employ to tap various candidate pools in terms of the willingness of the potential candidate to comply with the job requirements, the number of fresh perspectives and new ideas, the cost of training, and the average cost per hire.

3.3 Coaching and Training—Keep Your Team on Track

Communication is the nucleus of call center operations and proper etiquettes and protocols ensure that it is done correctly. Coaching and training for various aspects including communication need to be in place, and revisited and revamped on a regular basis.

Apart from telephone manners, CSRs need to be trained in the usage of formalized scripts. A formalized script is a to-the-point tool used to address customer issues. CSRs need to be trained in handling scripts so that they sound like they are reading it like a conversation; it should not sound like mechanical reading. Scripts should be used with the right tone and should get to the heart of the matter quickly. CSRs need to be trained in various other aspects of scripts like formatting and content. People need to be reminded time and again that scripts are mere tools for carrying out their operations, but what is more important are a great team, great training and a great working culture.

Thorough training, reward and recognition, and continuous mentoring are required to instill the qualities of anger diffusion, empathy, managing differences and taking ownership of calls.

Spotlight Tip
Coaching and training are generally a far more cost-effective investment than recruiting and retaining.

A call center manager needs to don many hats depending on the situation. As a coach, one needs to maintain a coaching journal, which one can update either on a monthly or quarterly basis. The journal should help one to guide one's CSRs in achieving the following aspects:

A. Immediate and Future Goals: Managers need to go beyond the incentive programs and delve in their CSRs' psyche to discover what really works to inspire and motivate them. Only then managers can train, coach and mentor CSRs in achieving their immediate and future goals. Only then managers can instill in their CSRs a sense of belonging and a drive to learn and grow with their organization.

B. Roadmap: Managers should use reporting metrics wisely. They need to use metrics to monitor their CSRs and their work patterns and practices. Based on these metrics, appropriate reorientation and improvement plans need to be formulated to keep them on the road to operational excellence.

C. Closed-loop coaching: Use "closed-loop coaching" to ensure that CSRs trust the results of such coaching. Each and every CSR is coached, measured and reinforced in a constructive, fair way. Equal criterion is applied to one and all. Results are communicated in real-time.

D. Changes in the workplace: Healthy changes like delegation, sharing of responsibility, mutual accountability and role rotation ensure that employees don't get bored of their routine work. Providing challenging changes and roles within the line-of-business or account help to develop personal competencies of the employees.

E. Motivating factors: Motivating the employees is important for maintaining the employees' morale. Given the tight deadlines, real-time service, volume of calls and many other challenging factors, it is crucial that the management compensates for the same, both monetary and in kind. Genuine praise, promotion and incentive programs are the best way of keeping the turnover rate low. Making feedback a two-way loop ensures that employees feel that they too are given equal importance and opportunities to influence the management agenda, just as their management has influence over their performance and recognition.

Sales communication is vital to the sales and marketing strategies of an organization. Training for handling communication in various sales-related scenarios is crucial, for example, communication between the sales workforce and sales manager or between one salesman and another salesman. This is necessary to avoid any sort of conflict of interests.

Special training needs to be imparted for handling irate and troubled customers. It is human nature to either give out a fight or flight reaction to angry remarks, but in call centers, such an irrational behavior is unacceptable. This training is necessary to instill alternative behavioral patterns in CSRs to handle angry customers effectively.

Since CSRs operate in various time zones, it is necessary for them to have a thorough knowledge of the time zones to provide effective, efficient round-the-clock customer service. Customers who reside in US live in nine standard time zones; managers of global call centers must therefore take into account these time differences while training their teams. In addition to these time zones, CSRs must also be made aware of how daylight time savings affect their work schedules.

Illustration 3.1: Spotless Round-the-Clock Service (regardless of time zone differences)

In today's era of a distributed work environment, call center managers need to design a mechanism for minimizing the influence of hierarchies and bureaucracies. They also need to develop ways of encouraging employees to connect to each other in this distributed work environment. In short, they need to provide direction, instruction, motivation and feedback.

3.4 Managers—The Source of Guidance and Support

A call center manager is the overseer of all operations taking place in a call center. He is the coach who is directing his team with adequate training and regular counseling. A call center manager needs to be thoroughly trained in order to manage conflicting goals of reducing staff turnover and enhancing staff performance.

As a call center manager, one needs to possess great communication skills to be able to interact effectively with several layers of the organization. And above all, managers need to be great role models who set an example for their agents to follow in the areas of empowerment, knowledge sharing, fair feedback, and setting clear goals and expectations. Managers need to adopt a facilitative style of leadership; they need to let CSRs be autonomous and creative in finding solutions.

Spotlight Tip
Call center managers are in a unique position to inspire their teams. They have the resources to create a culture of shared success, which helps CSRs to produce more positive results.

Apart from educational qualifications like a MBA degree and a good amount of working experience, a call center manager needs to exhibit the following skills and traits:

A. Coach, mentor and train employees. Being a manager of a call center, you should be able to bring the supervisors and CSRs together, and bind them to the organization's vision. As a team leader and mentor, a call center manager needs to adapt his behavior and approach based on individual work preferences and training needs. Personalized interaction helps to convince CSRs that they are as important as their organization's mission. Their skills and expertise are appreciated and needed for keeping their organization on the path of performance.

B. A manager should exhibit role model behavior through his words, decisions and actions. Decision-making and organizational skills are absolutely essential for managing people. Lead by example; do not lead by force or coercion. As a role model, a manager needs to be aware of the words he/she uses in various communication settings, for example, in the case of a personality conflict in the team, one needs to create a win-win scenario wherein everyone involved gets a fair chance to put up their views. One needs to create a culture of empathy where everyone becomes a support team to each other.

C. Escalate issues according to the procedures detailed out in an escalation plan.

D. Provide feedback in a transparent and honest fashion. A manager can adopt the "sandwich" method to share positive comments about an employee's performance, and then one can share constructive feedback, and finally end the feedback loop with yet another positive point. This approach ensures that the employees receive both appreciation and critical comments in a positive manner. Managers can use a whiteboard to highlight someone's stellar contribution each day; this form of public recognition is something that all CSRs cherish.

E. Front-line managers need to periodically take a recap of the baseline goals and performance benchmarks. This periodic scrutiny is necessary for them to make the required adjustments in team goals and roles.

F. As a recruiter, a manager needs to thoroughly scan the prospective candidates. A manager needs to possess a great psychological insight into human behavior so that he/she selects candidates that mesh well with the existing team and turn out to be team players eventually.

G. As an advisor, a manager needs to always maintain confidentiality of his team members and their concerns.

H. Managers need to ensure that their CSRs know they are a part of the corporate vision, not just a job profile.

3.5 Team Responsibilities—Mirror the Corporate Brand

When one thinks of call centers, one may only look at them as a means of answering calls, but there is more to them than meets the eye. They are about providing unrivaled support and mirroring the corporate brand promise.

The quality of the customer's service experience is directly linked with that of the call center employees' workplace practices and policies. Call center work is all about teamwork. The culture of excellence and motivation is a prerequisite to ensure that team goals and achievements are given importance over individual agendas. The spirit of collective responsibility is established and fuelled with mutual accountability and trust.

Empowered employees act as a cohesive team of *collaborative colleagues*. There are many strategies that can be introduced to bring about the best salesmanship and the culture of team excellence. Teamwork in call centers is the Midas touch for efficient Customer Relationship and Experience Management.

The location of the customers also determines the kind of responsibilities and roles a call center team handles. Working for the customers in US or UK needs you to be constantly upgrading your technology skills along with domain knowledge.

Team responsibilities include the following main functions:

A. Handle Calls: Apart from several tertiary functions like call routing, scheduling, planning, etc., the one main function which is done the most is dealing with inbound and outbound calls. Proper telephone standards and protocols need to be followed.

B. Customer Support: CSRs need to prove through their persistent efforts that the customers are the reason for their work, and not an interruption in their work. They need to give their customers personalized attention on first-priority basis, day in and day out. CSRs need to involve their customers in the resolution process as this goes to show that customers' interests are of utmost importance. By delivering professional, quality services before, during and after the transaction, CSRs prove to be a valuable asset to an organization's current and future success.

C. Reporting and Documentation: Collecting and analyzing data related to the customer interaction cycle is a critical piece in the call center puzzle. Analysis of this data not only helps to improve customer service, but reveals inroads leading to new markets. This is the reason why most call centers have a dedicated team of data analysts working on this data 24/7 to derive useful insights into growth and profit potential.

D. Sales Outreach: CSRs are responsible for establishing a two-way engagement between their organization and customers. They are responsible for creating a lead base through vigilant networking, customer demographics tracking and relevant advertising campaigns.

E. E-Mail and Chat Management: CSRs need to deal with e-mail and chat services in order to sort, manage, prioritize and respond to e-mail and chat communications.

F. Follow-up: In the case of calls gone wrong and dissatisfied customers, it is the duty of team players to deal with the rough patches. Options of automated follow-up do not work as disturbed customers mostly prefer to have live support and are willing to re-discuss with live resources only. As a team, you need to do all you can do to convert a disgruntled customer to a lifetime client. The team can also present a secondary offer to the customers in case the initial offer has been rejected by the customers in order to avoid a typical syndrome called *Buyer's Remorse*. It is a post-sales emotional state in which a customer regrets having placed an order/requesting a service. A premium in the form of a product or service that is positioned as a free gift within the context of an offer can help to win back the customers.

G. Confidentiality: CSRs need to maintain confidentiality and adhere to the terms and conditions of the non-disclosure agreement. It is the moral responsibility of the call center employees to ensure that they do not divulge sensitive information and intellectual assets like their work methods, customer data, business practices and leads.

3.6 Agent Retention—Recognize, Reward and Retain

They come, they go. You put lots of effort into attracting and retaining your customers, but can you say the same about your employees?

Organizations need to take all the required steps to ensure that the potential employees are fully aware of the working conditions and are given ample opportunities to assimilate themselves in the working climate. Organizations need to ensure that their employees are given opportunities to affect the financial bottom line favorably, for example, fair distribution of revenue-producing calls across the employee base guarantees employee loyalty.

An organization's first customers are actually its employees. When an organization's employees are happy in their working environment, they easily transfer these positive vibes to the external customers.

Repetitive working processes and patterns lead to boredom. This can be controlled with appropriate provisions. The staffing plan needs to include provisions for a productive work culture. A staff-friendly environment cuts down the attrition rate.

Working for a long stretch of time and dealing with unpredictable callers are bound to drain a person physically, mentally and socially. Having fun options like casual meetings, games and motivation camps help to retain agents and improve their well-being. These options help to keep CSRs doing their job and actually loving it as well.

To keep the environment agent-friendly and to reduce the rate of attrition, factors like an approachable executive team, motivating challenges, two-way appraisal systems, job diversity, and growth opportunities and new skills are some major provisions.

Both motivation and morale are important for maintaining a highly productive environment. Through observations and surveys, call centers measure the morale and motivation levels of CSRs. One important thing to remember here is that high profits may not be just because the morale and motivation levels are high; there is a possibility that CSRs are threatened, nagged or being micro-managed and this is not the right way of retaining agents.

Different factors motivate different people. Some are motivated by the sense of job security, some by better working conditions and some by the sense of contribution. There is a gamut of motivators that needs to be addressed.

Spotlight Tip
Human capital is the highest priority. Replace aggressive hiring and firing with comprehensive strategies to help call center agents to achieve their career goals.

3.6.1 Retention Strategies—Outside-the-Box Ideas

Managers along with executive inputs and employee suggestions need to design a foolproof retention roadmap. Innovative methods help in improving the agent engagement levels. The following outside-the-box ideas help you to increase agent retention:

A. Excessive control leads to agent attrition. A reasonable degree of accountability entrusted with CSRs improves the retention level; Focus groups are one such way of allowing CSRs to contribute to areas related to their work. Managers and supervisors need to nurture positive relationships with their teams, which help to offset the negative influence of organizational and departmental factors. Managers and supervisors who exercise a fair leadership style are most likely to retain their agents in a better way. Fair feedback, constructive environment, learning opportunities and equal participation in matters related to the agents' work lead to employee satisfaction and better performance.

Spotlight Tip
Managers and supervisors must get out of the need to control, and they will gain more control.

B. Developing a clear career roadmap for each of the employees is a must. Opportunities for lateral moves and promotions should be discussed upfront.

C. Conduct thorough exit interviews to capture the reasons of why people want to quit their jobs. Understanding why your employees leave is as important as understanding why they stay. These interviews guide the top management in making changes that reduce future turnover. Personal reasons or better pay are not the only reasons why agents leave. Poor management style and practices could be another area of concern and for which organizations can get firsthand feedback in order to implement timely damage control. If turnover is a problem—either because of the number of people who are leaving or the quality of people who are leaving sometimes using consultants to interview employees is a good idea, especially if confidentiality can be guaranteed. Many people will not actually tell their employer the real reason why they are leaving as they are concerned that it will affect references, etc.

D. Competitive salaries along with lucrative benefit packages (paid vacation, health coverage and flexi-timings) are needed to maintain a good work-life balance.

E. Make a provision to allow agents to work from home or anywhere they are comfortable working from. Leverage the power of technology to give them some degree of flexibility. It is about setting the right climate; it is about convincing agents that they are a part of a work-without-walls working environment. Many traditional outsourcers like Convergys have successful work-at-home agent models in place.

F. The workflow processes need to be assessed and revamped from time to time. Employee inputs also help to reconfigure the working climate, and in turn lead to higher employee retention. Seeking inputs from agents creates a sense of belonging and team spirit and makes them believe that their creative ideas are wanted. As agents know that their contribution is equally important in the betterment of their organization, this feeling of security leads to the sense of unique ownership.

G. It is human nature to avoid sudden changes. Change management is made manageable and less threatening in outlook by seeking active participation from agents. With proper management support and communication guidelines, change becomes acceptable to agents as they know that their inputs too are considered while introducing changes. A climate of trust and security is the key to retaining agents.

H. Training and retraining are a must. Surveys and studies have revealed that CSRs of call centers who are provided with extensive, ongoing training and retraining are more than twice as likely to stay back as compared to call centers that provide less training.

I. Creative ideas like having creative job titles make CSRs feel special. Have meaningful titles like "customer service specialist", "CRM expert", "transaction specialist", etc. Let employees use these creative titles on their business cards and e-mail signatures. They not only have a positive emotional impact on the employees, but also affect the customers favorably.

J. Job rotation and variation add the variety factor to the daily routine of agents, which in a way helps to promote the feeling of equal opportunity for growth and learning.

Destination: Call Center—Site Assessment

4

There are a plenty of sites that are call center-friendly, but the question is your call center eager to join these business communities.

Before you take your first call, you are going to have to find an appropriate site for your call center. Call center site selection plays an important role in the call center business cycle. Where a call center is located can make all the difference between its success and failure.

An ideal site is about maximizing productivity and profitability, and re-engineering the technology and human assets. A low-risk site plays a critical role in transforming a group of people from reactive fire fighters to *proactive performers*.

This chapter discusses various aspects like workforce availability, geographic location, competition, demographic makeup and many more in order to arrive at a balanced decision, which eventually helps call centers to meet their organizational goals and unique market needs.

By maintaining a great rapport with local economic development agencies and government authorities, organizations can smoothly sail through the zoning and application processes of site selection.

Before finding a new site, organizations need to also assess what has worked well and what hasn't in their current site by assessing their existing site specifications; these insights help to prevent repeating mistakes of the past.

To ensure an error-free decision, it is wise to hire services of a qualified site selection firm. Such firms normally assist organizations in all phases of site selection, right from the initial research to the finish-out process.

4.1 Organizational Mission—The Starting Point

Opening a new call center or relocating an existing call center...it all depends on the organizational mission. The purpose and the projected lifespan of a call center need to be ascertained. The organizational mission in terms of corporate goals, corporate identity and brand promise, customer needs, business objectives and success factors needs to be determined by soliciting inputs from all stakeholders. These goals, objectives and inputs are necessary for getting a buy-in on the site selection factors.

If your organization is well-known and is an employer of choice, then the perfect site is one that will help your organization to sustain this image of "employer of choice"; one that will uphold the corporate identity and brand promise.

For each of the site selection factors, organizations need to use market research, empirical findings, anecdotal evidence, and statistical analysis to get access to actual data, testimonials and experiences of existing employers, community colleges, local residents, and key market players like chambers of commerce, local economic development agencies, corporate investors, training facilities, etc. This statistical snapshot and competitive industry knowledge are required to reach a well-considered decision; one that resonates with the organizational mission.

To validate the data and information gathered from various sources, and to get a feel of the labor conditions, competiveness, operational flexibility and business environment, a designated team should conduct onsite visits to assess potential sites in terms of the various site selection factors, right from demographics to the Exit strategy. This team should consist of the key representatives from all departments, right from the executive component to human resources and from finance to marketing.

4.2 Labor—Requirements, Cost and Skills

The criteria of labor is about looking at the quality and growth rate of the various labor pools, and then matching them with the purpose of a call center. A site that provides a steady flow of workers to match to the size, growth potential and functions of a call center is a strong contender.

The target age group of the talent pool is one important factor in arriving at a balanced decision. For example, your target group is in the range 20-35, then an ideal site is one that has a higher than normal number of potential candidates in the 20-35 age bracket, this in turn results in lower turnover rates.

A site that has a sufficient level of qualified human resources becomes a critical factor in the selection process. The average level of education, language skills and computer literacy are key factors in determining the overall educational level of the workforce, and eventually in influencing a prospective site choice. Training costs are bound to be lower, if potential employees are already computer-savvy, are English-speaking and have good soft skills.

Factors like population growth, market growth, quality of life, number of new residents versus residents that are leaving, average household income level, seasonal requirements, underemployment and unemployment rates, and the type and number of personnel available play a crucial role in site selection.

The way an organization wishes to organize its personnel plays an important role in site selection too. For example, distributing staff across buildings within the same site based on their skills; this scenario needs in-depth analysis on several points like number of buildings, costs, labor pools, etc.

The health and overall well-being of employees should be given priority-one importance. Availability of nearby health facilities is a major deciding factor. Factors like natural calamities and seasonal illnesses need to be thoroughly analyzed in order to ensure business continuity. Other nearby community resources and civil facilities like restaurants, libraries, hotels, parks and recreational centers are a plus.

A clean and crime-free environment is another aspect that organizations need to study in order to take care of their employees' health and safety.

The sources of labor pool from which a call center recruits are important too. For example, if a particular call center needs graduates for entry-level posts, then selecting a site where there is a strong presence of local colleges is beneficial.

Unionization issues—a site with a highly unionized market may not be suitable. An extreme "us vs. them" mentality may not be that call center-friendly.

Retail trade in the form of malls, shopping centers and stores is a significant aspect as this aspect makes it easier for call centers to find trained and experienced professionals in the customer service domain.

The work site needs to be a pleasant and interesting place as this factor keeps the employee engagement level high and the turnover rate low.

All the above factors are necessary to short-list a site where there are enough prospective employees to support call center operations over the immediate horizon and in the long run too.

4.3 Time, Monetary and Infrastructure—Handle with Prudence

Site selection is a time consuming process so organizations need to plan this process upfront. In fact, they need to include site selection as a major component in their business plan. The gestation period of a call center needs to be taken into consideration while drawing out a plan for site selection. The time frame of starting a call center and the time frame for completing the site selection should be vigilantly matched.

As real estate prices soar, maintaining an in-house call center may be a costly option for small-sized organizations. Instead outsourcing these services saves them not only space but money too.

Monetary resources in terms of initial investment, build-out costs (in the case of own facility) and cash cushion reserves majorly affect the selection process. If an organization does not have a strong monetary muscle, then it should look for rented sites or sites that offer leasing with an option to buy.

Monetary investment is justified only when a particular site demonstrates the ability to generate substantial interest from the target customer segments in the concerned organization's products and services. Sites with a track record of market responsiveness are a great option.

When choosing a site, organizations need to remember that call centers heavily rely on high-speed networks, telephony connectivity, communications architecture, telecommunication facilities, and software solutions and hardware components. So there is no point in selecting a low-priced site if the reliability and quality of these infrastructural components are low. This tradeoff is a dicey one and needs to be handled with prudence. Don't let real estate considerations overshadow critical factors. For example, if an organization handles customer service through VoIP technology, then there is no point in selecting a site that comes at a cheap price and is not VoIP-driven. Another major aspect to consider is whether the sites have infrastructural components that can provide for a greater scale of operations, for example, distributing and coordinating work across geographic locations.

The work timings are very important in determining the kind of utilities and infrastructural facilities a call center needs. Round-the-clock call centers need to study the site for the availability of cost-efficient standby power systems, UPS back-up facilities and power feeds to handle outages.

Vendors and suppliers of services—potential sites need to provide reasonable access to top-ranked vendor and service provider networks that most closely meet a call center's needs. Organizations need to evaluate vendors' and suppliers' capabilities and portfolios in potential sites. Vendor interoperability is another key measure that needs to be analyzed.

4.4 Taxes, Time Zone, Safety and More—Objective Focus

Taxes on telecommunications services play a major role in finalizing a viable site. At times, even locating across the street can lead to a substantial decrease in the tax burden. Legislation in terms of taxation, incentive packages, exemptions, training grants, telemarketing laws and right-to-work laws needs to be studied before finalizing a particular site.

Organizations need to educate themselves about the various economic development benefits available in the contending sites. An objective comparison of potential sites from this perspective helps organizations to pinpoint more strategic sites, which will help to increase corporate welfare.

Time zones play an important role in call center costs. If a particular call center is planning to operate in the normal shift, then additional costs won't come into play. But if a call center has night and graveyard shifts, then the shift differential pay factor adds to the overall call center costs. In such cases, an appropriate geographical location plays a critical role in minimizing such costs.

Positive attitudes of local people, access to health care facilities, development agencies, cost of living, security measures, transport options, etc., need to be present in order to have a stable working climate.

Many people prefer to pursue a part-time degree or course while they are working. Sites that provide access to local vocational institutions and colleges are sure to attract more people.

A site with reasonably predictable weather conditions is another consideration to be studied before finalizing the call center location.

Linguistic capabilities—a dialect neutral location is a great option as it allows seamless service to the customers across the globe. Global call centers will benefit a lot from sites that provide them with constant access to a bilingual and multilingual talent base. For example, if your call center is going to deal with English-speaking customers and German-speaking customers, then it needs to be in a place where there is a large number of English and German speakers.

As call centers operate across time zones, they tend to remain open longer than other types of industries and sectors. Due to this reason, they require additional cost-efficient electricity and robust security.

It is always better to select a site which has less or no competition. When the type of business and skills of your call center are different from other call centers, then your call center can coexist with other call centers in the same area. A low saturation level is always better.

A site with scalable utility services like water, sewer system, etc., is more likely to be short-listed.

Airport access, rail access, well-connected roads and reliable means of public transport are a must for reducing commute time. Less travel time equates to less traffic issues like traffic jams, irritation, etc. This in turn translates to better moods of the employees.

If your call center caters to employees with special needs, then disability-friendly practices and measures must be supported by potential sites.

Political stability is necessary for long-term growth, and such sites are more attractive than others.

In the case of leasing, organizations need to examine the structural soundness of buildings and premises. Factors like quality of electrical works and power points, building materials, load bearing capacity, floor layout and design, air conditioners, lifts, fire alarm systems, etc., need to be carefully studied before negotiating and finalizing lease contract terms and conditions.

The related services dependent on call centers are training, transport, catering and security services, and vice versa. Availability of and accessibility to these auxiliary services is a must for both of them to survive and to add to the economic development of their respective organizations.

4.5 Space Requirements—From Start to Peak

How much space is needed at the start of operations? How much space is needed at the peak of operations? The answers to these important questions are needed to determine whether potential sites have the required acreage to accommodate present and projected future needs.

When a call center hits the perceived physical capacity limit, shifting or expanding may not be the only reason for more space. There could be other factors like underutilization of current resources. Such possibilities need to be identified first, and only then the decision to find a new site should be taken.

Expansion plans are an important deciding factor as they guide you in selecting a site which you can add space to later on when you witness further growth or ramp-up. Whether a call center builds from scratch or hires new space or goes in for the build-to-suit option, it all depends on the expansion plans. For example, if an organization is planning to open a new call within 3-5 months, then the lease option is the most suitable option. Based on these points, organizations need to negotiate reasonable terms and conditions with real estate developers.

The long-range perspective of growth and expansion is essential. Conduct a planning exercise that provides a 3 to 5 year growth projection in terms of life span and operational requirements. This projection helps to select and design the office space in the most suitable manner. Design flexibility is the key factor.

Office space size in terms of headcount, site shape, number of floors, individual floor space, size of actual usable area, on-site and off-site parking space, recreational center, and other spaces needs to be calculated in order to determine what kind of a site will be short-listed—Own, Lease or Build-to-suit.

4.6 Site Selection—Potential Choices

The perfect site is vital as it involves huge investment in terms of resources, both human and money. This worksheet helps to avoid pitfalls by focusing on critical selection factors.

The various aspects discussed in this chapter need to be scored or ranked. Relative weight is given to the sub-factors and then a composite score is derived by adding the scores of all sub-factors within each category to determine the relative importance of the main categories. Then you add up all the category totals to derive the final score, which is then used to narrow down the choices to three to four sites that most closely match the goals and success factors. Further analysis and site visits are required to make the final selection.

Category—Organizational Mission		
Sub-category	Relative Importance	Observations, Comments
Business Objectives		
Corporate Goals		
Customer Needs		
Corporate Identity and Brand Promise		
Category Total:		
Category—Labor		
Sub-category	Relative Importance	Observations, Comments
Quality and Growth Rate		
Target Age Group		
Type and Number of Personnel Available		
Average Level of Education, Language Skills and Computer Literacy		
Population Growth		
Average Household Income Level		
Turnover Rate		
Sources of Labor Pool		
Underemployment and Unemployment Rates		
Health Facilities		
Business Continuity		
Unionization issues		
Seasonal Requirements		
Category Total:		
Category—Time, Monetary and Infrastructure		
Sub-category	Relative Importance	Observations, Comments
Gestation Period		
Real Estate Prices		
High-speed Networks		
Telephony Connectivity		
Telecommunication Facilities		
Software and Hardware		

(Contd...)

Standby Power Systems, Power Feeds and UPS Back-up Facilities		
Monetary Muscle		
Vendors and Suppliers of Services—Capabilities, Portfolios and Interoperability		
Category Total:		
Category—Taxes, Time Zone, Safety and More		
Sub-category	Relative Importance	Observations, Comments
Tax burden		
Exemptions		
Right-to-work Laws		
Telemarketing Laws		
Economic Development Benefits		
Time Zones		
Attitudes of Local People		
Access to Local Vocational Institutions and Colleges		
Linguistic Capabilities		
Competition		
Political Stability		
Utility Services		
Airport Access, Rail Access and Well-connected Roads		
Category Total:		
Category—Space Requirements		
Sub-category	Relative Importance	Observations, Comments
At the Start		
At the Peak Level		
Growth Projection		
Office Space		
Design Flexibility		
Category Total:		
Final Score:		
Add all the Category Totals to get the Final Score: Recommended Site > 75 Final Score Marginal Site 50-70 Final Score Poor Site 0-45 Final Score		

5 Careers—Avenues of Progress

If you are looking for a job that will give you flexible hours with a great salary, then the call center field is the right choice. A career in the call center field is a lucrative opportunity. As call centers are needed by most industries, right from manufacturing to banking, there is ample opportunity for both professionals and non-professionals to get into this space.

Call centers are a craze among youngsters for the career mobility and the hefty five-figure salary that they offer. Educated graduates and undergraduates have access to a wide variety of openings. With growth-driven opportunities come certain challenges like odd hours, irregular eating habits, health issues, etc. But with proper guidelines and measures, such challenges can be handled well.

5.1 Preparation—From Interview to Appointment

Before hiring call center personnel, an organization must conduct thorough screening of the candidates through a battery of tests, interviews and discussions. These days, organizations are more likely to consider a candidate who has a high school and college level diploma or a degree in English, information technology or business management. Potential candidates need to take the time to research the desired position and call center in terms of its clientele, style of operation, service and product offerings, etc.

A great covering letter is something that will get you started on the right path. Spend ample time in preparing the covering letter and make sure it clearly reflects your understanding of the position and the call center you have applied for. Your résumé should highlight your skills, especially customer interaction experience, and showcase how these skills can help the concerned organization in achieving its goals. Both the covering letter and résumé are a great way of marketing your personality traits, confidence level and skills. KSA—knowledge, skills and abilities are the key factors in acquiring a job and continuing to perform it well. KSA is a cluster of unique competencies that one needs to perform a job in accordance to the job definition/task statement.

The basic prerequisites that you might have to improve before applying for a call center job are as follows:

A. English Proficiency: You also have my book on the importance of the English language in today's world of globalization, *English Language: The Gateway to Global Growth*, to guide you on the path to preparation and progress.

B. Call center communication is a skill that needs a lot of patience. Handling irate customers needs patience and empathy. At the same time, when things get out of hand, one needs to have vigilance to identify and escalate priority issues.

C. Soft skills like confidence and the knack to handle varied personalities are a plus. Laser-sharp listening, an extrovert nature and the ability to multi-task are a great combination.

D. Anticipating and dealing with odd situations is a part and parcel of the job profile. Real-time management of all sorts of issues is also necessary.

E. Though training for job and organization-specific policies and procedures is imparted, possessing basic prior knowledge of the same is a big plus.

F. Some call centers prefer hiring people with sales experience. If you have a track record in sales and marketing, then you definitely have an edge over the others.

Anticipating and handling interview questions plays a big part in the selection process. Here are a few likely questions that you need to be prepared for:

A. What software skills do you possess? Are you proficient in handling computers?

B. Tell us about your previous experience in the call center space. Narrate at least one difficult customer service situation and how did you tackle it? Such behavioral questions help the employers to gauge the candidate's stress-tolerance level, problem-solving skills and other behavioral competencies.

C. Do you consider yourself as a team player?

D. What do you think goes into making a successful call center?

E. What are your weaknesses and strengths? This is a standard question applicable to all professions. It is particularly crucial for a call center job interview as this is a people-oriented field. The employers are interested both in your people skills and professional skills.

Be wary of the way you give answers as the interview sessions serve a dual purpose: 1) to check your competency and skills. 2) to scrutinize your body language, verbal cues, language and grammar skills.

A Word of Caution
There are call centers catering to the needs of various industries, right from finance to health care. For a better career and growth prospects, you must select the one that suits your qualifications and interests the best.

As a potential candidate, one should have prior knowledge of what roles/duties a call center employee performs. The main responsibilities of a call center employee are:

A. Handle calls in a professional manner.

B. Resolve customer complaints/requests based on thorough analysis of the knowledge database.

C. Possess thorough knowledge of organization's products and services.

D. Respond to customer inquiries promptly.

E. Persuade potential customers to purchase a product or service.

F. Follow-up on initial customer interaction.

G. Generate customer leads.

5.2 Qualifications—Both Academic and Soft Skills

Regardless of experience, age, caste or gender, the call center domain is one such option that has a lot of space and opportunity for one and all.

The top three questions to which you need to have answers to when applying for a job in a call center are:

A. How good is my communication and confidence level?

B. Do I possess the required soft skills like customer-centricity, patience and empathy?

C. Am I comfortable with the usage of modern tools and technology?

Once you are equipped with answers to these questions, you then have the qualities that recruitment managers highly appreciate.

The key competencies that an organization looks for in the applicants are:

A. Problem analysis and solution

B. Team player attitude

C. Communication skills

D. Writing ability

E. Customer service orientation

F. Listening ability

G. Potential to make soft or hard sell

H. Good typing skills

Call center employees play an important role in addressing customer requests and issues, something we all know as problem-solving. This essentially means that potential candidates need to have proven analytical skills to handle job pressures effectively and meet the demands of a fast-paced professional life.

Call center job applicants need to have a great mix of written communication and verbal proficiency. In global call centers that cater to both English speaking and non-English speaking clientele, it is seen that bilingual jobseekers in particular, enjoy excellent opportunities and growth.

Usually CSRs require good typing skills; an average of 60 to 70 words per minute is beneficial.

A basic level of comfort with CRM databases and telephony systems that the organization uses is also a plus. A good candidate is also aware of the CRM practices and principles in terms of showing courteousness, maintaining confidentiality, etc.

In certain cases, cultural background could also be one of the parameters for short-listing candidates. For example, a call center catering to Mexican customers would prefer agents with this background.

There are so many things that go into the making of a successful CSR, something we all refer to as a *multi-tasking* professional. As a CSR, you need to handle several factors simultaneously, right from handling computers and keyboard shortcuts to troubleshooting complex problems and interacting with the customers.

Spotlight Tip

Look beyond the veneer of job objectives.

A proper mindset coupled with a host of soft skills like communication, problem-solving and a customer-oriented attitude is what will help you to highlight your résumé.

5.2.1 Call Center Skills—A Quick Recap

Call center skills are categorized based on the various job positions available in call centers, and which we have discussed in detail in this chapter. Some of these skills are needed to be selected by call centers and some of these skills are developed through coaching, mentoring and training. This cluster of competencies ensures that employees grow and learn as the business grows. Here is a quick checklist of skills needed to do well in call centers:

A. Communication skills: Cover a gamut of competencies like culture-specific knowledge, objective and sincere give-and-take of information, and active listening skills. Language skills become all the more important due to globalization of transactions; they give you the ability to understand and be understood across cultures.

B. Problem-solving skills: Potential candidates need to have the analytical and critical thinking abilities to resolves a caller's issues quickly and conclusively.

C. Technical skills: As call centers are modern setups, employees need to be proficient in handling the systems, right from dealing with the Internet to navigating complex databases.

D. Sales skills: Ability to provide quality sales and service on each and every call by demonstrating in-depth product and service knowledge, satisfying customer needs and managing calls in a professional manner.

E. Basics of telephone manners and netiquettes (in the case of web-based call centers) are needed to ensure smooth operations. They are needed to enhance the customer experience and customer satisfaction levels.

F. Soft skills: Skills like positive work ethic, ability to handle non-verbal cues, reliability, time management, team building, dependability, adaptability, accountability, personal integrity, flexibility, business awareness and willingness to learn.

5.3 Growth Opportunities—Several Openings

Today, call centers are a multi-billion dollar field. A career in call centers is something more than just another business catchphrase; this is a great space to get exposure in the global economy.

High pay packages, an environment where a well-rounded personality can be achieved and an opportunity to be part of an upscale, globalized work culture draw many to call centers. Call center employees come from varied backgrounds. There are several openings for college students, freshers, seasoned professionals, retired people and homemakers in the posts of call center executives, virtual office assistants, trainees, offshore customer care specialists, chat support executives, call center operators, quality analysts, supervisors and managers. There is a wide range of options when it comes to choosing to work in a call center. In fact, many people join call centers at the entry level with an aim of moving to other departments later on.

It is widely known that the career graph is growth-driven and fast upward moving as compared to any other industry or sector, especially at the entry level. There are many other opportunities in a call center other than the position of a CSR. Trainers are an important position as call center training is critical. Team leaders, supervisors and managers are needed to coach, mentor, appraise and guide the personnel. Consultants and analysts are needed to make the right business decisions, forecast various trends and derive statistics. Other related departments like workforce management, hiring, training, research and development, sales and marketing, and quality control and assurance are a source of great openings for experienced call center professionals.

Lateral entrants and experienced professionals can take up roles in the front-line positions or they can don supervisory and managerial hats or even join higher posts in other departments.

Cross-function training and experiences are another significant area of career diversification whereby call center employees get cross-trained in other groups like web support, technical support or collections within their own call center. This option helps them to decide whether they want to continue in their current role or move into other groups.

After gaining 2-3 years of call center experience, one can branch out to other roles like process managers, team managers or leaders. Managers, supervisors and trainers typically begin as CSRs and are promoted through the ranks over time and can take up roles of increasing responsibilities such as product manager or marketing manager.

Even during downsizing and the economic downturn, call centers are the least affected. The reason is simple—the level of customer needs goes down due to low monetary power to buy goods and services, but it is still present (though at a much lower level) and customer needs are still there to be taken care of. Thus, CSRs are not as vulnerable as employees in other fields.

A career in call centers exemplifies the concept of "Earn While You Learn", which empowers the student community to finance their own education-related expenses and also gain international exposure in the corporate world at such a young age—dual advantage.

Call center career fairs, job avenues and association meets are a good way to create networking and to enter the professional space. As one gains experience, one moves up the ladder in the call center domain by taking up managerial or supervisory roles. Another career path that opens up is that of venturing into other departments like research and development, where employees apply their thorough knowledge of products and services for improving the quality of existing products/services, for designing new features in the existing products/services and for introducing new ideas.

Often you will find that organizations have other departments like training and quality housed along with their call center facility. As these are all housed in the same premises, it is possible to learn skills related to these different departments, which in turn expand the talent base.

Many organizations have call center branches located throughout their country and this helps employees in relocating themselves without having the fear of losing their jobs. Again this aspect depends on the transfer policies of organizations.

For individuals over 35-40 years of age, Teleworking is a great option. Teleworking/Telecommuting is catching on fast as a new way of working because of its flexibility factor. It tailors the nature of work to suit the worker's needs, and it offers flexibility in work location and timings. Integrated Services Digital Network (ISDN) and Internet Protocol (IP) networks have facilitated the growth of Teleworking. It refers to work done from a remote location instead of at an organization's premises—Mobile Telework, Telecenters, Satellite Facilities, Home-based Telework or Remote Office Centers.

Most call centers prefer to promote employees to management positions from within the organization itself. This gives CSRs ample opportunity to prove their mettle and develop a progressive career graph.

Often global call centers have offices located in developed nations like USA and UK, and they send their employees to these locations for acquiring a better understanding of the workplace dynamics and for seeing the world through different eyes. Apart from the increase in know-how and exposure to a whole new culture, these employees also get a chance to earn more.

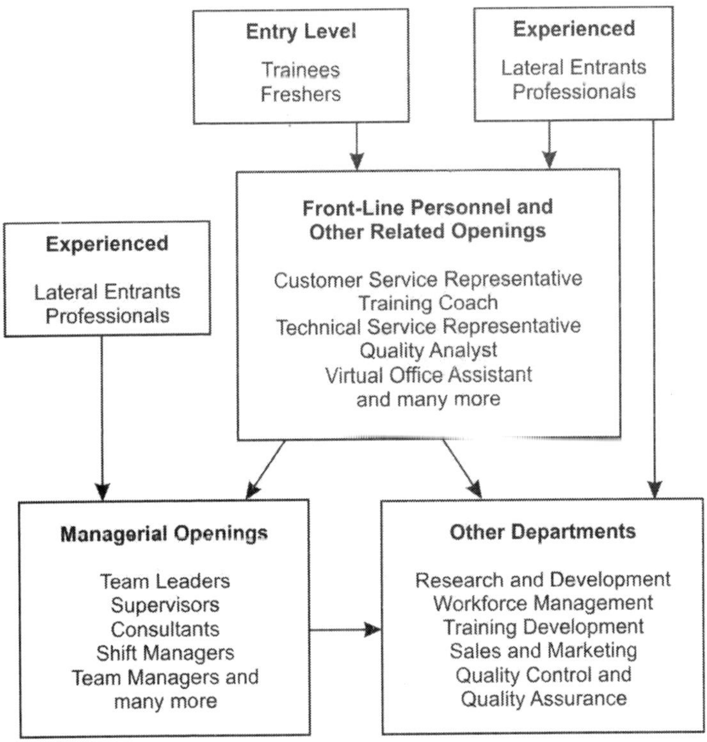

Figure 5.1: The Call Center Career Path

The call center environment provides you with ample opportunities for continuous learning; it provides you the impetus to do better each day. There is always an opportunity for self-improvement.

Now more than ever, the call center space is maturing in terms of creating new advancement options and career paths.

5.4 The Downside—Challenges and Remedies

Working in call centers is quite challenging and stressful; it is synonymous to performing a juggling act in a circus. As a call center employee, one tends to be knee-deep in work. What is required to perform well even under pressure is reserving a few minutes for personal thinking and self-reflection (you can do this as soon as the phone stops ringing). Self-reflection helps you to pinpoint the reasons for your stress and once you know the reasons, you can work out appropriate stress-relief strategies. My book on personal transformation, *The 6 Spheres of Life: Unlocking the Door to Success and Happiness*, helps you to realign your emotional landscape with the demanding lifestyle of call centers.

What will you do as a CSR when the customers say statements like: "Well can you tell me how to start the thing needed to connect to the Internet" or "Are you through with your processing. So now you have time for my issue finally". These unnerving statements put you under great pressure, but what is needed is a bit of preparation and common sense to deal with irate customers. Organizations need to have comprehensive procedures and practical training for improving customer contact and care. Clear guidelines regarding how such calls should be reported and when they should be terminated are needed to lower the level of stress. Short breaks should be allowed to CSRs who have just taken an abusive call to recover from the incident.

Employees are likely to face threats, insults, harassment, abuse and injuries from teammates, supervisors and managers too. Employers must implement security measures to ensure the protection of employees from such serious issues. It is important for management to get involved and solve such problems by having an open door policy. Coping skills and training need to be imparted in order to instill positive behavioral patterns of sensitivity, empathy, active listening and mutual respect. Organizational checks to eliminate faulty behavioral patterns and mindsets are needed. For example, a manager who makes an exception for his favorite team member should not be entertained at all. Clear-cut guidelines related to dignity, respect, equal and fair treatment, and correction measures in the case of abuse and harassment need to be issued. Consequences of not following the organizational guidelines should result in reassignment, disciplinary action or penalty, and in worst cases removal from job.

CSRs need to be made aware of the various work-related safety guidelines as they are as much responsible as their organizations are about their health, dignity and safety. Both CSRs and organizations need to hold health and safety in high regard. Adequate safeguards of their dignity, honor, safety, and their transportation to and from their homes is a must, especially in the case of women employees. Advanced tracking mechanisms like Global Positioning System (GPS) can be used to keep track of transportation vehicles' locations.

Working in a call center results in a drastic change in one's natural biological clock. With odd working hours, graveyard shifts and a high work volume, health hazards like high blood pressure, severe headaches, eye strain, depression, insomnia, repetitive stress injury (RSI happens when too much stress is placed on a certain part of the body, for example, in the case of call centers, overusing the hands to perform a repetitive task like dialing or typing), and other stressors like acoustic shocks and blurry vision are likely to hamper the health of call center professionals. Organizations are not only responsible for their employees' economic stability, but are equally responsible for their social and emotional health, and mental fitness. Organizations need to have on-campus doctors and counselors who take care of these health issues in a timely manner. Safety and health representatives should be hired and workplace safety and health committees should be formed by call centers to bridge the gap between employees and top management. This is necessary for identifying and minimizing risks from hazards, injuries and incidents. Emotional, social and spiritual health can be maintained through employee wellness programs, workplace wellness promoters and wellness newsletters. These options help to build a culture of community and support groups where each and every person in the workplace knows that his health and overall well-being is a top priority. When organizations invest wisely in their employees' wellness, they are definitely going to succeed in lowering health care costs and maximizing employee productivity.

Dealing with unreasonable performance demands and competing goals and that too in a repetitive and machine-like fashion makes working in call centers mechanical and employees may feel that they are simply another component of the technology setup. Stress management techniques need to be included in the training programs in order to prove to the employees that they are much more than the technology they work on; they too are an integral part of the corporate agenda. Suggestions schemes, checklists, feedback sessions and walk-through inspections are needed to give employees a platform to express their views (both negative and positive) on the elements of work.

At times, organizations may decide to start outsourcing to other countries like China or India. In such cases, there won't be any work for the original CSRs unless there is an option for relocation. This uncertainty creates a sense of insecurity, feeling of betrayal and loss of identity within the workforce, which may lead to illness, high blood pressure, depression, etc. Both organizations and employees need to work together to deal with the uncertainty associated with possible or actual job loss as a result of outsourcing, restricting or downsizing. Employees can turn to their home support system for psychological comfort. On the professional level, employees need to start networking, seeking advice from various sources of knowledge, and retraining and upgrading themselves in order to work out a career makeover. Employees can look at this situation as a way of fulfilling their long nurtured dreams. This period of uncertainty is a good time for honest self-appraisal and reassessment of professional goals; employees can utilize this time for identifying where their true passion lies. Group bonding and group therapy are a great way to cope with this factor. Top management can help by providing complete support for such group vent-out sessions and leading their precious employees through change. Transparency is the key to coping; management needs to be transparent in sharing all the relevant information so that the employees can enhance their chances of survival and personal control. Organizations need to arrange coping workshops that encourage employees to share and express frustrations, and also provide collective resources to move forward in life.

A huge percentage of the workforce is young people. Call center operations get monotonous by the day; people calling and at times even yelling and more people calling and yelling. This cycle puts the workers in a bad mood, especially the Generation Y, which in turn causes fallouts in the personal space as family members and friends may not be able to handle such workplace-related tantrums. There is practically no time between calls to recover from an irate customer or customer rejection. Here stress-relief programs, team de-briefings, and a social approach where employees diffuse their anger and strain through laughter and jokes come to their rescue.

Call center jobs are sedentary in nature and this leads to several problems like obesity and laziness. Exercise or practice yoga for about 15-20 minutes daily and that should keep you fit; a gym area and recreation facilities like a TV room, pool table and team outings help to recharge employees. Organizations need to make provisions that encourage employees to vary postures and have movement in their workflow, for example, modifying tasks and giving 'time out' breaks not only provide on-the-job exercise, but also grant a reasonable degree of control over the workflow to the employees. Employees can perform stretching and joint mobilization exercises during breaks.

Due to odd working hours, CSRs tend to pick up wrong habits and addictions. CSRs are heavy coffee drinkers and smokers as they believe that coffee and smoking help them to stay awake at night. But this is a myth! The healthy *mantra* is to follow a healthy diet and lifestyle. A good intake of water is a must for relaxing your throat and larynx, and for preventing voice and throat irritation.

Child care is another important aspect that employers need to provide for. For employees with small children, organizations need to provide an on-site child care and child activity service or should ensure that there is a day care center nearby. These facilities lessen the worry level of employees, substantially. Employees feel comforted as they are in close proximity to their children even while at work and can visit their children in their off-work time. A combination of an employee-centered culture and a child-centered attitude proves to the employee base that they along with their families are highly valued by their employers.

Poor lighting causes eye disorders and soft tissue injuries arising from the adoption of awkward postures. Organizations must provide adequate lighting and illumination. Factors like shadows, reflections and glares need to be eliminated in order to ensure work continuity and prevention of eye strain.

Another major aspect of an ergonomically sound office setup is that of the emergency exits; they should be designed to enable quick and safe exit in emergency situations so as to minimize injuries and accident rate.

Temporal mobility and physical mobility are two important aspects that need to be provided for by call centers. Adequate facilities for traveling to work and from work need to be in place. Especially in the case of women, safety should be the top most priority of organizations as this helps women CSRs to adapt themselves to the transformation from "safe at home" to "safe at work before, in and after the night shift". Though times are changing (at a slow pace), women still face social issues, both at work and at home for being a part of the call center nightscape. Call centers need to strictly follow comprehensive safety guidelines to prevent women from abuse and hostility. Organizations need to provide security gadgets and mobile phones to women employees with pre-programmed features that enable them to send messages to their office or local police in emergencies. On the brighter side, due to economic stability and a good pay package, women are becoming more independent, confident and empowered.

Organizations must ensure employees are not exposed to a degenerative or oxygen-deficient atmosphere by providing adequate air conditioning and ventilation. A proper air flow and a comfortable temperature level are necessary.

As CSRs are in close proximity to the headsets, infections of the ear and mouth are very common. Organizations need to have a regular cleaning and maintenance mechanism in place.

Employee fatigue is another downside, but with proper measures and controls, fatigue can be minimized substantially. Due to fatigue, employees become irritable and commit errors in their job, and can also cause accidents due to lack of alertness and reasoning. Fatigue also increases the absenteeism rate and leads to sleep disorders like insomnia. Organizations need to reduce all sorts of fatigues—cognitive, vocal, physical and visual. Cognitive fatigue can be handled by avoiding the trap routine; employees can uplift their moods by having quick chats of 5-10 minutes with their colleagues or can use the techniques of meditation and visual imagery to zone out negative thoughts from their mental landscape. Employees and their managers need to set achievable priorities and goals, and work out reasonable workloads in order to ensure that employees do not develop cognitive incompetency. Measures like installing sound masking devices, minimizing background noise, and providing volume control and acoustic shock prevention devices on headsets can prevent voice misuse and ear pain. A reasonable level of automation is a big plus. For example, agents can record repetitive message like greetings and upload them into the system so that every time a caller calls they are played automatically. No matter what problems agents are facing, callers still get to hear a personalized, cheerful greeting due to automation. Equitable distribution of calls is another way of ensuring that no single agent's voice is overworked or underutilized. By offering additional rest periods, implementing shift swapping and reviewing overtime schedules, organizations can help employees to reduce their physical fatigue levels. Physical fatigue can be relieved through progressive muscle relaxation; the cycle of contracting and relaxing the various muscle sets helps to release muscle tension. Visual fatigue can be handled by taking one minute of rest for every 20 minutes spent on the computer screen and by maintaining a reasonably good blink rate. Relaxation exercises and shifting of focus from near-by to far-away objects can help to relax the eye muscles. A perfect display screen contrast is necessary to minimize visual strain.

As CSRs deal with sensitive data related to the customers, they are required to operate in a highly regulated environment. In order to eliminate all possibility of data theft, employees have to leave all their personal belongings in lockers before they enter their cubicles. Some CSRs may find these working rules as derogatory. The simple trick to overcome this feeling is by placing yourself in the customer's shoes or by recalling your own call center experience where you were the customer.

Employers need to provide a productive working environment where all the required amenities are in place, right from drinking water and first aid to ergonomic arrangement and washrooms. Employees should be able to move freely to and from these amenities and other work-related areas without facing inconvenience or obstruction.

Apart from the above stressors, CSRs may have to deal with personal insults and racist remarks from international customers. You cannot make everyone happy. Answering nasty callers should be handled in the following ways:

A. Do not snap back. Listen to the customer with patience.

B. Listening with patience pays off as the customer's anger cools down after sometime.

C. Once an aggressive customer calms down, you can hope for a constructive communication cycle. After the call is over, CSRs can make faces at colleagues to diffuse stress caused by angry or abusive callers, or share a joke or two to lighten up the environment. Such social approaches are very useful.

D. Some customers just want to rant out their aggressiveness and do nothing more than that. In such cases of crank calls, CSRs issue warnings and then press the 'crank call' button to block the numbers of such customers.

A Word of Caution
Working in a call center is not about glamour and a lot of money; it is about a lot of patience and a positive personality.

A simple trick that works wonders and transforms a bad mood into an upbeat one is to forget the negative side and concentrate on the following positive points of working in a call center for a few minutes, on a daily basis:

A. An environment that provides the opportunity to enhance interpersonal and negotiation skills.

B. An opportunity to test and refine skills.

C. 24/7 exposure to the global business arena.

D. An environment that allows one to accept and incorporate constructive feedback to improve performance.

This exercise helps to overcome the daily grind and instills a renewed sense of determination to carry out the call center tasks in full sincerity and integrity.

Organizations need to constantly review workstations, redesign jobs, work schedules and tasks, and revamp the environment to ensure hassle-free operations.

Organizations, government agencies, local authorities, industry experts and employees need to work on the issues in unison, and provide timely and adequate information, training and guidance to the employees.

Table 5.1: Dealing with the Downside

Downside	Measures
Work pressures and competing goals	Self-reflection, checklists, stress-relief strategies, suggestion schemes, feedback sessions and walk-through inspections.
Irate and abusive customers and co-workers	Diffuse anger and stress through a social approach, listen with patience, short breaks of recovery, concentrate on the positive elements of work, open-

(Contd...)

	door policy, coping skills and training, and methods of correcting and punishing faulty behavioral patterns and mindsets.
Health hazards, injuries and the safety of women	Safety guidelines, community and support groups, on-campus doctors and counselors, employee wellness programs, wellness newsletters, safety and health committees, and workplace wellness promoters. Vehicle location tracking and security gadgets for women employees.
Monotonous and sedentary work	Team de-briefings and a social approach, 'time out' breaks, task modification, and yoga and exercise. Opportunities for participating in the development of workplace policies and procedures.
Child Care	On-site child care service or a nearby day care center.
Eye disorders and soft tissue injuries	Adequate lighting and illumination, and removal of factors like shadows, reflections and glares.
Fatigue, irritability and accident-prone work	Background noise reduction, acoustic shock prevention devices, equitable distribution of calls, automation of repetitive tasks, additional rest period, meditation, visual imagery, achievable priorities and goals, good blink rate, progressive muscle relaxation, perfect display screen contrast and continual refocusing.

Despite all the odds faced in call center workplaces, CSRs enjoy a gamut of employment benefits in the form of:

A. Performance Bonuses, both cash-based and noncash-based in nature. They help to keep CSRs motivated and engaged for a long time. Examples of cash-based bonuses are individual, team-based and spot bonuses. Examples of noncash-based bonuses include gift certificates, free lunches and travel vouchers.

B. Pension Plans

C. Fixed Cash Benefits, for example, meals and transportation allowance.

D. Life and Health insurance

E. Differential Pay, for example, Shift Differential pay is paid to employees who work in a shift that is different from the normal schedule.

F. Intangible Perks are those little fringe benefits that make a big difference in easing an employee's work life, for example, flexible work timings and a reserved parking space.

G. Discounts on organization's products and services.

Call center management needs to encourage employees to report issues and participate in the development of workplace codes of practice, procedures and policies, and at the same time, also ensure that follow-up by supervisors is done to close these gaps, minimize occupational hazards and prevent motivational meltdown. A safety-first corporate attitude, an ergonomics-friendly work environment, and policies that provide a workspace and work conditions suited to employees' age, goals, preferences, special needs and capabilities always facilitate call center employees to focus on the positive aspects rather than the downside.

5.4.1 Litmus Test—Employee Inputs Work Wonders

The following worksheet helps employees to determine whether or not their working climate is employee-centric. Their responses assist organizations in developing employee-friendly working conditions, codes of practice, policies and procedures.

Employee Name:

Please answer the following using options Yes or No:

A. Are suggestions schemes, checklists, feedback sessions and walk-through inspections in place for you to share your feedback on work-related factors?

B. Are proper instructions, safety guidelines, health programs and practical training provided?

C. Are there policies and procedures for handling personal insults, and bullying and abusive behaviors?

D. Are there provisions to deal with ergonomic risk factors?

E. Are employees consulted on the workplace design?

(Contd...)

F. Are emergency procedures in place?

G. Are risk control measures in place?

Please rate the following aspects on a scale of 1-5, 1 being Not At All and 5 being Very Satisfied. You can also include any comments, suggestions and observations along with your ratings.

Aspect	Rating and Comments/ Suggestions/Observations
Guidance, Information and Training	
Is guidance related to hazards, risks and mitigation strategies comprehensive and to what degree is it helpful in your job?	
How satisfied are you with the information and instructions provided to you regarding health and safety measures?	
Is training regular and are you satisfied with it?	
Amenities and Workstation Design	
How happy are you with the amenities—water, recreation, food and first aid?	
Is the lighting and ventilation adequate for performing your job in a safe manner?	
Are the workstations designed to suit your needs, movement and duties?	
Is there is enough working space? Is there enough storage space?	
How easy is it to access all the amenities from your workstation?	
Safety and Health Measures	
How satisfied are you with the safeguards provided for safety, dignity, honor and health?	
How happy are you with the on-campus doctors and wellness programs?	
Are the stress-relief programs and social approaches able to diffuse your stress and anger levels?	
Job-related Factors	
How happy are you with the options for overcoming the ill-effects of a sedentary job?	
How satisfied are you with the design of your work procedures and job tasks?	

(Contd...)

To what extent is smooth movement and degree of control over work facilitated through task modification and time out breaks?	
Customers and Co-workers	
How happy are you with the procedures and techniques to deal with angry customers?	
How satisfied are you with the methods implemented for correcting and punishing faulty behavioral patterns and mindsets within the teams?	
How happy are you with the coping skills and training to handle irate and abusive customers and co-workers?	
Ergonomic Factors	
How happy are you with your desk in terms of leg space, height adjustment, surface top (non-reflective) and desk width?	
Are the chairs ergonomically designed in terms of free movement, backrest, height, body posture, seat pan width and depth, and elbow space?	
Are the headsets cleaned on a regular basis, equipped with noise control features and replaced when faulty?	
How comfortable are you with the workspace provided for your furniture, documents, workstation and equipment?	

Please rate the following factors on a scale of 1-5. 1 indicates lowest and 5 indicates highest.

A. How successful are you in being able to balance your personal and professional life?

B. Are you quick enough to identify and report loopholes in the implementation of working procedures, policies and codes of practice?

C. How successful are you in being able to deal with unreasonable performance demands and competing goals?

Additional comments about how the management can improve the strategies for dealing with the downside:

PART-II

Staying On the Path—Customer Experience Excellence

In this part...

The unique theory of superior customer-focused experiences—*The Wheel of Nurture* is described here.

This part deals with the *CARE* formula and experience drivers, which provide the personal touch and human insights to overhaul customer experience management.

It also discusses the supporting factors for the theory in terms of customers, performance, communication and tools.

6

The Wheel of Nurture Theory—Care for the Customer

Do you ever wish you had a crystal ball that could predict how your customers are going to behave and how long are they going to remain loyal? Well, both you and I know that such crystal balls don't exist, but with the guidelines given in my theory—*The Wheel of Nurture*, call centers will know for sure which levers to pull to provide top-of-the-class customer-focused experiences; something that I call *Customer EDGExperiences*. These levers are the various experience types that call centers have with their customers along the experience maturity curve.

Each one of us is born with a basic nature; it is something that is governed by inherent factors like our upbringing, biological traits and psychological makeup. But there is one other external element that is constantly playing its role in shaping our personality, experiences and behavioral patterns—NURTURE; it is a gamut of environmental factors. Just as parents of a young child or infant provide him/her with a nourishing environment of emotional and physical security in the form of well-being, medical care, love, affection and proper nutrition, similarly, call centers need to take care of their customers by nurturing them and their experiences.

Our actions and behavior fall into two main categories. Some behavioral patterns are driven by genetic predispositions while some behaviors are a result of various conditioning factors. These conditioners are something that call centers need to capitalize on to ensure customer service and satisfaction. We will be referring to these conditioners as nurturers or better still as *experience drivers*.

This theory has two parts that make the customer experience equation complete:

Optimize the CSRs' schedule leading to reduced costs + Optimize the customers' experience leading to increased returns = Optimized Customer EDGExperiences

To solve this equation, this theory and its supporting elements describe the pertinent experience drivers that condition the customer's mindset, behavioral patterns and attitudes, and enrich the customer experiences from various angles. It all starts out with an economic bond which focuses on the monetary gains of both the parties, call centers and their customers. The next stage is that of a knowledge bond where both the parties strive to improve the experience maturity through communication, knowledge sharing and knowledge learning. Once reasonably good comfort and trust levels are established, the customers are motivated to continue this journey due to a social bond. And the final stage is that of a psychological or emotional bond. To maintain a positive orientation of the customers in all these bonds, the various experience drivers come to the fore.

6.1 CARE—The Heart of the Theory

Although automated tools can perform a lot of the call center operations, it takes personal touch and human insights to overhaul customer experience management. The heart of this theory is CARE. CARE is the formula for top quality customer service and customer focus in call centers. It is about *building experiences around the customers*.

The *Oxford English Dictionary* defines the word care as "the provision of what is necessary for the health, welfare, maintenance, and protection of someone or something." We do a lot of personal-level nurturing for ourselves and our family, but as thorough professionals if call centers do it for their customers too, then this is what I call Value-based Nurturing. Value-based nurturing refers to the practice of developing shared values (monetary and emotional) with the customers through committed partnerships. Just as consistent experiences, mutual trust, strong ethics, collaboration and reciprocal attitude are integral components of nurturing in our social sphere and personal lives, in the similar manner, they play the exact same role of fostering ethical behavioral patterns and positive mutual growth in the corporate world. Just as elders teach their family members the values of trust, commitment, teamwork and sincere feedback, in the similar manner, call center leaders should foster an environment of value-based nurturing for the customers. This nurturing is something that will transform experiences into bonds of commitment, where both the call centers and their customers co-create honest and rewarding customer experiences.

CARE stands for the following experience drivers:

A. **C**ommunicate: Interact with the right customers at the right level in the right way and at the right frequency.

B. **A**dapt: Adapt processes, people, tools and technologies to bridge the gaps identified during interactions.

C. **R**eflect: Think and re-think about the level of willingness and readiness to relate to the customers in order to overcome any mental blocks.

D. **E**nable and Engage: Collaborate with the customers to solve their problems and to incorporate their suggestions in products and services. By proactively engaging the customers, call centers are able to create a strong brand affinity. Call centers need to enable their customers by constantly coming up with new ways and channels to engage the customers with their brands.

Each of these drivers maps to the various experience types. It all begins with learning and then moves on to growing, commitment, and finally emotional affinity. Initially all the experiences are transaction-dominated, but as one moves forward on the experience maturity curve, the experiences become driven by mutual trust, knowledge sharing and collaboration. As the experience level matures, so does the customer loyalty level—this is how the customers climb the ladder of loyalty.

The basis of these drivers is value-based nurturing. As call centers and their customers move through each of the drivers of the customer care cycle and venture one step further on the

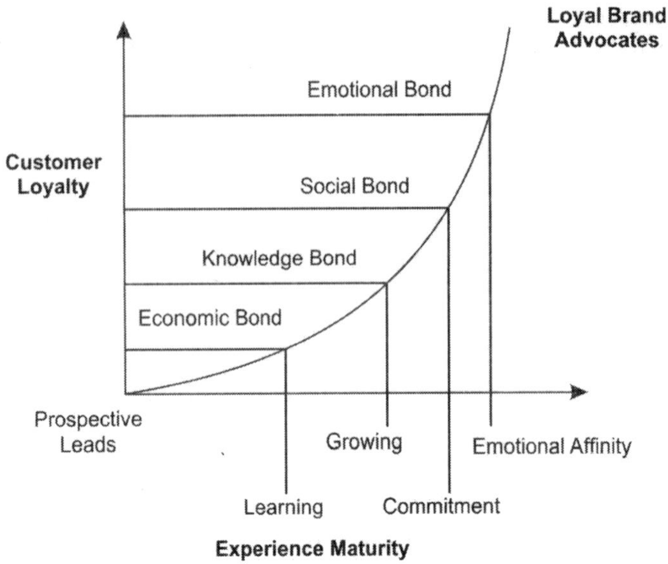

Figure 6.1: The Customer Experience Maturity Curve

experience maturity curve, the level of commitment and affinity between the two is bound to increase, and finally it leads to steady sales and revenue streams for call centers and steady streams of satisfaction for the customers. This growth is analogous to the growth that we all experience in our personal lives when we work in unison with our family members, friends and relatives.

6.1.1 Communicate—Learning Experiences

By communicating through cross-channel dialog with the customers on a constant basis, call centers develop a strong sense of awareness of the customer context; this context forms the basis of customer experiences. They are able to capture significant information bits and then organize them into coherent information reserves—Customer Intelligence. Call center teams need to constantly act on this information flow and analyze the same, and then apply the learnings to enhance future customer experiences. This process is cyclic in nature and is necessary to maintain an effective flow of communication and a *learning* experience between the customers and their call center. By leveraging different channels of communication, call centers can increase their visibility across different channels; hence making it easy for new prospects to find them.

Once call centers identify their customer goals and make them a part of their corporate agenda, they will know how to take CARE of their customers too. Call centers need to nurture their customers by creating a shared language for transmitting key information and messages to and from the customers. Gone are the days of bombarding the customers with one-directional information, now are the times when the customers get to choose the information that's relevant to them. In other words, all interaction should be customer-initiated communication. The key is to interact at the right level in the right way and at the right frequency; the main aim is to make interactions as rich and interactive as possible by delivering personalized innovative content to the customers.

Just by thinking ahead of the customer needs and expectations, organizations can make their customers feel taken care of. Customer focus groups is a great tool to capture the Voice of the Customer (VOC) in terms of their unique needs and expectations, and then using these insights for building stronger relationships with the best customers results in reinforcing an organization's brand for a lifetime. This in-depth, personalized probing of customer characteristics helps call centers to get answers to questions like what type of experiences to offer, how long are the experiences likely to last, and what kind of motivational investment to make to optimize these experiences.

Call centers need to create opportunities for communication so that they can build a strong database of customer information, and at same time, also educate the customers about their latest offerings, policies, incentive programs, etc.

The Learning Experience through the Communication Driver facilitates exploration and awareness of the customer context.

6.1.2 Adapt—Growing Experiences

First-time customers need to be pleased as their perception of the value that they derive from the entire experience journey is something that will drive repeat business. First-time customers equate to long lasting impact. In the case of repeat customers, merely 'show me that you know my needs and demands' concept won't work; call centers need to reinvent the wheel by designing new techniques, tools, processes and people management strategies of personalized care and knowledge-sharing. Right from business processes to workforce optimization, everything needs to be adapted to the customers.

In all cases, call centers need to be proactive in using new tools and channels to drive up the customer value. Call centers need to move beyond loyalty-incentive schemes, reward programs, bonus clubs and loyalty programs, as the customers of today find these terms to be cheap marketing gimmicks, and moreover, in such schemes, clubs and programs, customer loyalty is for the incentives, and not for the brand.

How to care for the customers and their new ways of communication? The answer is to *social network* with the customers. Yes...this is the age of the *Social Customer* and *Social Customer Experience Management*. Organizations need to do a thorough study of what all social media options do their customers prefer, and then adapt the best combination to serve their customers.

By demonstrating the ability to differentiate and customize offerings, call centers can ensure that their customers do not feel obligated to buy, but rather feel cared for.

All the above points are about sharing value with customers in proportion to their value—Shared Values, both in monetary terms and nurturers. Call centers need to mirror the congruity in their goals with that of their customer interests. This in turn results in the customers identifying with their call center brand; only then the customers take pride in being associated with a particular brand. Brand loyalty and shared value are strongly connected with each other. Building a brand in collaboration with the customers gives them a sense of partnership as they know that their suggestions, knowledge and inputs are a valuable element of the innovation process. Collaboration nurtures the ability of existing customers to be able to share their brand experiences with other customers thereby increasing overall brand awareness.

Spotlight Tip
The customers can help build your brand, only if you let them. Research has proved that half of the brand value is contributed to by customers.

The Growing Experience through the Adapt Driver creates a definite corporate-level identity for the customers. This identity is one of the main antecedents of increasing customer loyalty and also decreasing the price sensitivity factor and the concern for future welfare of the customers; hence higher purchasing frequency, raised purchasing intent and enhanced customer value.

6.1.3 Reflect—Commitment Experiences

Make the happy customers happier, and help the-less-happy turn into experience-rich customers. This drive to deliver consistent and involving experiences is something that drives the commitment level from the customers' side and evokes relevant customer behavioral outcomes too.

The customers, like children, must be cared for, protected, nurtured, and not to forget pampered with goodies—in our case, customer-focused experiences is the solution.

Call centers need to inculcate the art of reflection in their employees; it should become second nature for employees to learn from their interactions and observations from customer contact cycles in order to close any gaps. Only then the customers will reflect their brand-experience loyalty through their attitudes and behaviors, and continue their relationships with call centers.

The Commitment Experience through the Reflect driver creates a committed relationship. This committed relationship when enhanced by drawing insights from lessons learned results in the Confidence AdvantEDGE—customers feel less anxious and more secure to give their exclusive involvement in an evolving experience journey with their call centers.

6.1.4 Enable and Engage—Emotional Experiences

Call centers can be true care-givers and nurturers only when they create experiences around their relationships with the customers. For this to happen, call centers need to look beyond the veneer of volume-driven metrics. For example, Average Talk Time and Average Handle Time are commonly used metrics where the talk time is given importance. This theory encourages call centers to use novel and forward-looking metrics like Average Interaction Time and Average Nurture Time. These are to do with human insights and personal touch of handling customers by employing human aspects like empathy, cultural sensitivity and understanding to develop rich, unified, proactive,

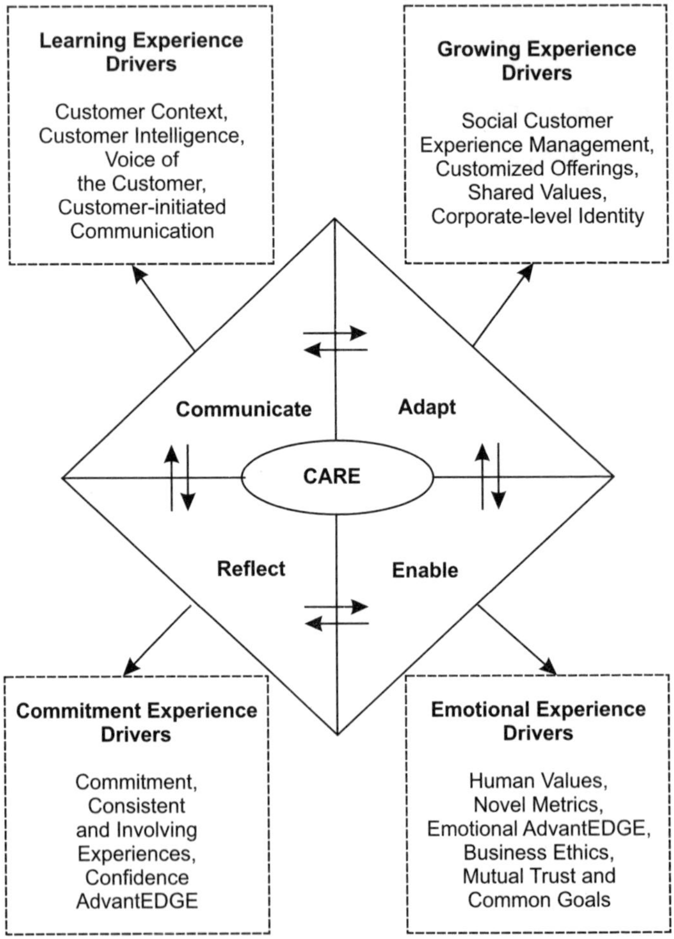

Figure 6.2: The CARE Diamond

meaningful multi-media experiences. These soft metrics provide insights into the customer brand attitudes and experiences. These insights facilitate the development of appropriate customer engagement strategies.

Enabling the customers is true nurturing and it is not merely about cheap, in-the-face marketing tricks. Relationships and experiences are built on the foundation of human values of trust and integrity—Emotional AdvantEDGE. Over time, as the customers have more and more reliable, well-connected experiences with a certain product or service, their relationship focus shifts from the product or service to the underlying call center emotional drivers in the form of business ethics, mutual trust and common goals.

Engaged and empowered customers are the least expensive to service. Call centers need to constantly monitor parameters like the level of feedback provided by the customers and their frequency of interactions in order to ensure the inclusion of right techniques of engagement, both offline and online mediums. A judicious mix is necessary to progress on the path of enablement and engagement—awareness, consideration, inquiry, purchase and retention.

The Emotional Experience thorough the Enable and Engage Driver builds a community of hard-core advocates.

6.2 The Wheel of Nurture—Inputs and Integration

Call centers are the locus of customer focus. In several organizations, call centers are the main arm of providing services to the customers. This fact shows that customer care and service provided through call centers has a great impact on the overall growth of such organizations.

The most precious resource of the customers is time and providing time-saving services to the customers is the call centers' most precious gain. This theory is about connecting these two facets to achieve optimized Customer EDGExperiences.

Formal strategies, tools and methods are needed to foster customer loyalty, but even before these aspects, the one main factor that needs to be in place is the culture of customer focus.

Organizations that provide world-class customer experiences always concentrate on the basics.

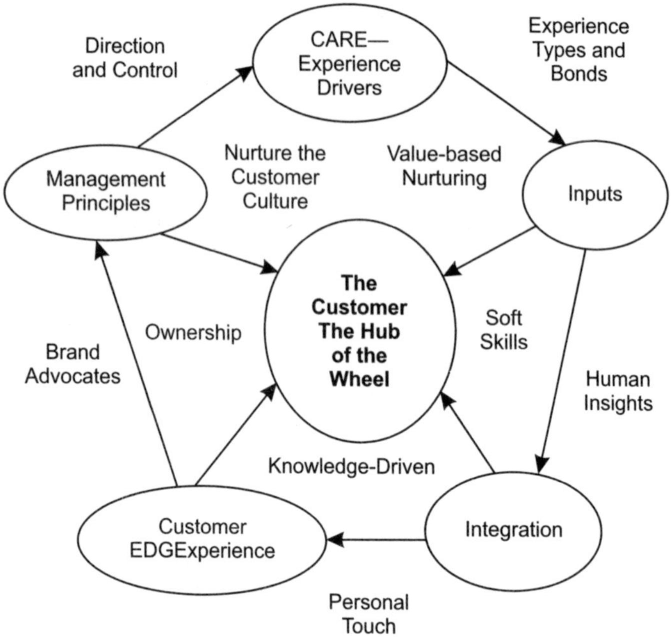

Figure 6.3: The Wheel of Nurture

Customer Focus is the ultimate package of care. There are three aspects to achieving customer focus and ultimately call center success—Inputs, Integration and Customer EDGExperience. For each of these parts of the equation, there are experience drivers which are already covered in the previous subsection, plus these equation parts and experience drivers have full-fledged chapters dedicated to them in this book. The core and advanced management principles needed to keep all these aspects in place so as to instill *Nurture the Customer Culture* are explained in detail throughout this book.

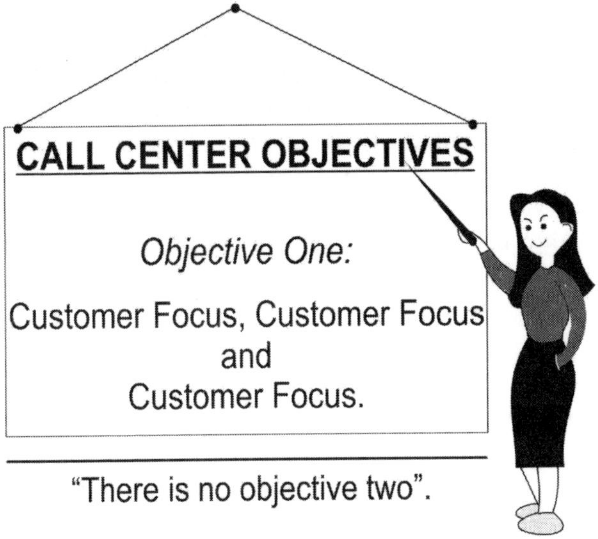

Illustration 6.1: The One and Only Objective—Customer Focus

6.3 The Balancing Equation—The Nurture Center

Each of the experience drivers of the CARE finds a central place in the equation components of the theory given as follows:

6.3.1 Inputs—Human Insights

Inputs are indicators from the customers' end that help to answer one of most important strategic questions—'what exactly do the customers want and need?' Each and every decision should be taken with the customer impact in mind.

The customers provide inputs and feedback only when they find that the front-line personnel exhibit a high level of honesty. Honesty is being as good as your word.

Self-reflection is also an important aspect for molding the mindset of CSRs in order to increase their level of willingness to relate and adapt to the customer needs and expectations.

The executive component needs to give CSRs ample opportunities to increase their own as well as the customers' level of engagement and empowerment.

Forecasting customer demands based on past customer data, anticipated future figures and employee feedback is one aspect of keeping customers happy, but what really keeps them coming back is "soft skills"—conditioners like genuine concern for customer concerns, empathy and politeness. The customers keep coming back to organizations that care for them. They give firsthand feedback on products and services, which in turn fuel the motivation levels of CSRs. Call centers need to measure and observe customer behavioral patterns for insights, which in turn help to increase the Occupancy/Agent Utilization. It is the percentage of time that agents are actually handling calls versus waiting for calls to arrive.

As the customers are driven by social media, it is best to nurture their needs through this very media. Organizations need to adopt social media features and tools that are most popular among their customers. Organizations need to analyze factors like whether the customers like blogs, photo-sharing sites, forums, etc., so that they can tap these tools to attract the customers.

CSRs need to be both persistent and friendly to identify new leads and prospects. Maintaining sincere follow-up shows a high level of persistence. It is crucial to be in touch with the customers on a regular basis.

Customer relationships are more than a mere "sales pitch". Relevant and timely interactions lead to solicitation of relevant and timely inputs. The customers are the most authentic source of direct constant market reaction. Customer context and customer expectations are constantly changing and to gauge them, organizations need to constantly keep in touch with their customers to find their satisfaction level in various areas like business ethics, technical support, distribution flexibility, etc.

Active listening and communication skills combined with a recording system are a must for making improvements in the experience management cycle as transparent a manner as possible to the customers.

6.3.2 Integration—Personal Touch

The second most important question to answer—'what do we need to do to be able to produce and deliver to our customers?' This is where integration comes into play. Integrate and calibrate what is required and what is done during each step of the customer communication cycle in order to improve the quality of each and every transaction and add a personal touch to each and every interaction.

Combine the findings, observations and learnings from various sources of inputs into a coherent body of knowledge to adapt to new situations, customer needs and experiences. The customers value their experiences with organizations that are knowledge-driven. The customers truly believe that their experiences with organizations are of value when call center employees possess unique, competitive knowledge that can add value to the customer experience cycle. More than just integrating knowledge reserves, it is about 'integrating the customers into the corporate culture'. It is about process maturity and people improvement.

Just as we all constantly integrate interactions and observations into a body of coherent knowledge from our daily routines and learnings so that we can nurture our personalities with the right factors, similarly, CSRs need to get into this habit. Thinking ahead of the customer's needs is crucial. It is about nurturing your channels of reaching out to the customers.

This integration is necessary in order for the customers to repose their confidence and trust in call centers. Only when CSRs exhibit behaviors that are consistent and predictable over time, the customers are ready to continue with the relationship building process. It is about aligning organizational goals with that of the customers through knowledge reserves.

6.3.3 Customer EDGExperiences—Customers Own Them

By being truthful about products and services, both in terms of positive qualities and negative points, and also by showing the willingness and competitive capability to overcome the negative points, call centers are able to ensure that the customers feel more reassured of having EDGExperiences. Call centers need to let the customers know that they own the relationships and experiences.

Research studies reveal that 55% of the customers are willing to recommend an organization due to its outstanding service and experience, more so than the price or products and services.

All these aspects empower call center management and CSRs, and with the right tools and knowledge, they can transform the customers into sincere advocates of their call center. Loyal customers are the most effective means of marketing. Customer loyalty goes way beyond financial gains or departmental success. Customer loyalty achieved through this theory ties back directly to the bottom line.

This theory provides call centers the building blocks of sustained competitive advantage, which take the call center performance to the next level, from customer satisfaction to customer loyalty. The Wheel of Nurture theory along with its supporting elements helps call centers to address the new realities of customer experience management successfully.

The Customers—The Heart of Call Centers

7

Today, the customers demand that organizations provide the same or higher level of service as the last organization they went to...and this applies to call centers too.

Call centers are in the people business. Front-line staff has the power to make a tremendous difference in the customer's experience. The customers are more likely to remember one bad customer service experience than they are to remember ten good ones. Counting calls is important—but it is even more important to make sure that *every* call counts. Remember, bad news travels faster and farther than good news. Loyal and happy customers share their positive experiences with about 4 to 6 people. Imagine the kind of positive word of mouth publicity you would get if you keep your customer base happy!

An unhappy customer: "I won't complain and I won't come back too".

Or

A happy customer: "Excellent service provided! I will keep coming back".

It is evident that the first response is the one which all organizations want to remove from their system. The second response is what this book is all about.

The customers are central to organizational success. Every second online business portal and print magazine highlights the importance of customer satisfaction. Do and measure everything from a customer's perspective in order to enhance the brand equity. This chapter enables your CSRs to develop a customer-oriented approach towards their work.

7.1 More than Just Calls—Commitment to the Customers

The customers are always right and they expect to get continuous support. Call center services operate in a 'live' environment and it is the first and foremost duty of CSRs to attend to their customers. Only then the customers spread positive word about call center products and services.

It is important to keep in mind that attracting a new customer costs 5 times as much as retaining an existing one. The customers must be treated with integrity and respect.

According to the estimates from the American Management Association (a corporate training and consulting group), 65 percent of an organization's business comes from repeat customers. In other words, your customers make or break the transactions.

Treat your customers as you would like to be treated. The customers need to be made 100 percent sure that catering to their demands is the most important goal for a call center.

Spotlight Tip
The more professionally organizations treat their CSRs, the more professionally these CSRs treat their customers.

7.2 Experiences and Relationships—Customer-Centric

What gives one call center an edge over another? Where do you think are the biggest opportunities for improvement? The answer is *Best-in-class Customer Experience*!

Call centers are a critical component of a successful customer experience and relationship management strategy. Customer experience and relationship management have moved to the forefront of call center goals. In the new business climate, I would say "Customer Experience is the King".

The customers are buying the experiences, communication channels and relationships that organizations are promising them, and not merely their products or services. The 21st century is considered as the service industry century. Customer satisfaction and service quality are closely interconnected.

Call center mission statements have gone from "meet the customer expectations" to "exceed the customer expectations".

'Act and sound professional' is the key *mantra* of a well-managed call center.

Right from business consultants who are responsible for maintaining a happy customer base to HR managers who are responsible for recruiting the right people for expanding this customer base have to define their work and policies around the customers and their needs.

Illustration 7.1: CEM is the Key to Success

Although the big picture is important here, don't undermine the importance and the role of the customer in the big picture. Customer experience management (CEM) is an important aspect for adding value to customer relationships. It is even bigger than customer relationship management. Traditional CRM systems are more concerned with fulfilling an organization's goals, whereas CEM systems strike a balance between the corporate agenda and customer satisfaction. CEM is about providing a unique experience, which in a way is an effective brand building exercise in itself. Self-serving practices erode the customer base; it is best to adapt organizational efforts to the customers rather than asking them to adapt to organizational efforts. CEM has become so important that new roles like chief experience officer are being introduced solely dedicated to handle this aspect.

According to a recent study (2009) conducted by Forrester Research (a technology and market research company), 89 percent of organizations consider customer experience management as a crucial component for success. This essentially means that all decisions and changes in a call center begin and end with the customer in mind. It is about "qualitative" thinking.

Customer experience and relationship management help to ensure that CSRs, technology, customers and processes work in unison. CEM and CRM help to integrate all the working groups in a call center. For this integration to work well, there are three main areas that a call center needs to give its 100 percent commitment to:

A. Customer listening can be achieved by energizing call center teams continually. Creative tips like adopt-a-customer or communicate with counterparts in other call centers help to develop tools and processes to improve customer management. Communication is central to all relationships. It should translate into the following points—providing services as promised, and in a prompt manner, at the promised time and for the promised value.

B. Collecting feedback and analyzing customer behavior to adapt processes accordingly. Customer feedback helps call centers to understand from the customers' point of view of how and what a call center is performing in order to exceed customer expectations. At the same time, the customers also feel that they have been heard. Prompt follow-up lets the customers know that you not only 'listen' to their feedback but also 'act' on it.

C. Catering to the new needs and trends based on the customer behavior helps to create and maintain brand loyalty. It is about the willingness and readiness to respond to the customers.

Spotlight Tip
Not all customers are important. Well-managed call centers are about identifying the right customers and their true value to their organizations.

The choice of CEM and CRM software is a crucial one. It needs to be done in line with your business functions and customer experience and relationship management goals. Specialists can help in analyzing the various options and selecting the *optimal* solution. Another important aspect is that of customizing the software to suit the business needs. The customers of today are highly demanding; hence the chosen software needs to be scalable too.

It is a good practice for call centers to share customer feedback and monitoring data with other departments within their organization in order to improve customer satisfaction and trust levels. Integrating data and findings from various sources of customer statistics like competitor analysis, surveys, call center logs and reports, user groups and customer profiles helps to smoothen out the entire customer management cycle.

7.2.1 Customer Analysis—The Top 20 Percent

It is essential to truly understand and anticipate customer requirements to develop a successful marketing strategy. This is where customer analysis steps in. It is the process of identifying and determining the customer psychographic profile, demand dynamics, socioeconomic status, motivation, needs, cultures, value drivers, lifestyles, buying trends, behaviors, reference groups, service support preferences, purchasing patterns and the likelihood of additional purchases by bringing in data from various sources. This data is then converted into actionable information to improve offerings and long-term customer loyalty. It allows organizations to identify and target the most profitable customers. The top 20 percent of customers represent the high-value segment and they contribute to 80 percent of the revenue. The purpose of this process is to identify this top 20 percent.

There are three sub-processes involved in this process—analysis before the transaction, analysis during the transaction and analysis after the transaction. Before elements like total market size, socioeconomic status and location are analyzed. During elements like purchase value and motivation are studied. After elements like satisfaction level, propensity to recommend and chances of repeat purchase are analyzed. By drilling down this data, call centers gain insights, visibility and granular information about various dimensions—channels, new markets, retention, etc. These sub-processes assist call centers in finding answers to the following questions:

A. Why do your customers choose to connect to your call center?

B. Which are the high-value customers? How much effort it takes to keep them satisfied?

C. Where do you stand in comparison to your competition in terms of quality, pricing, delivery, etc.?

D. What are your customers' buying motives?

E. Which market segments/niche areas to focus on so that you retain your existing customers and add new customers too?

With answers to these questions, call centers are able to develop optimal offers, design segment-wise marketing channels, predict future behavior of their customers and gain many more insights on various dimensions. This business intelligence helps to capitalize on market potential, to profile the key attributes of the customers, and to calculate the current and future value of the customers.

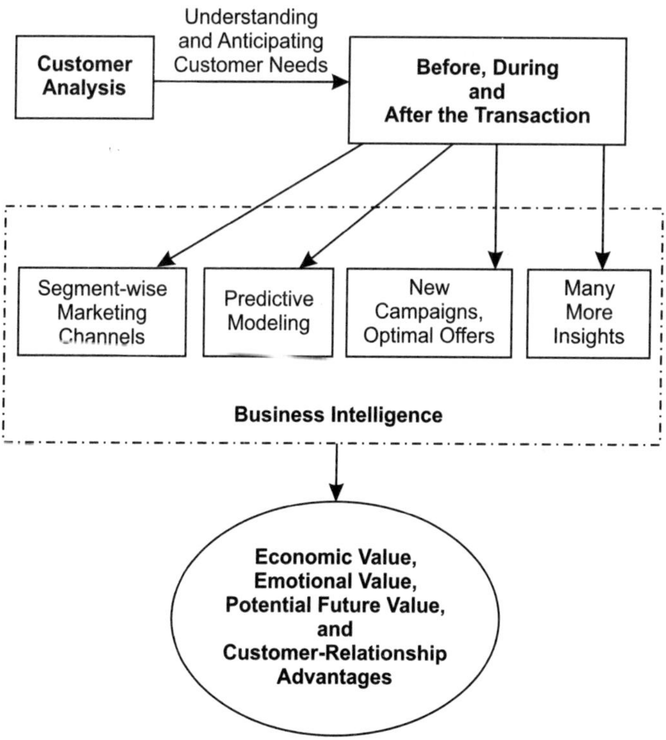

Figure 7.1: The Customer Analysis Flow

For this process to be a success, continuous monitoring of customer interactions is required. The processes of data collection, mining and analysis are iterative in nature. The main purpose of this cycle is to assist call centers in providing the apt solutions to customer issues by using minimal resources.

7.2.2 Processes—Remain Customer-Focused

To grow your business, you have to grow your customer loyalty. The ancient Chinese proverb "To serve is to rule" says it all. It is about giving loyalty (to the customers) before loyalty is received (from the customers). The entire customer experience life cycle, right from the brand promise to the actual experience management is about recognizing, engaging, serving and growing the customer base.

The main aim of customer-centric processes is to let the customers go away satisfied instead of just going away. They also help managers of call centers to identify and fill in the gaps in call center processes. With the help of social media and social networking, dissatisfied customers cause trouble for call centers that do not provide them with up to the mark service. For example, the customers can use social networking websites to share their dissatisfaction of a particular product or service with their friends and colleagues. If CSRs vigilantly watch such sites to track information and feedback regarding their products and services, they can use this very same public platform to resolve customer grievances, and that too in real-time. Call centers can increase awareness about their products or services through social media and social networking sites. This kind of public platform-oriented customer service scenarios need to be trained for.

Leading call centers believe in building processes that keep not only their CSRs but also their customers well-informed. This approach helps both internal and external customers to prepare for and accept changes.

Customer satisfaction is an important metric for measuring whether products/services are meeting customer expectations and needs. It also helps to determine the customer's satisfaction level with regards to the quality aspect. Processes, practices and policies to handle this metric help in establishing a firm working relationship between the organizational agenda and the customer service aspect.

Value-based segmentation is a critical component for keeping the customer base intact. It is the process of segregating the customers based on various marketing factors like spending patterns, age, type of calls, size of business, etc. This division helps call centers to formulate appropriate marketing strategies to cater to the various target groups. Customer and call segmentation is on the rise as the customers are becoming more demanding, both in terms of requirements and the value they attach to a product/service.

A comprehensive customer feedback process needs to be in place in order to measure the customer satisfaction level. Call centers need to look beyond immediate service level satisfaction. Finally, at the end of the day, it is about customer retention. According to studies, a 5 percent increase in customer retention can increase profits by 25 percent to 95 percent. The feedback process must cater to the following aspects:

A. Business objectives

B. Customer objectives

C. Visibility into your customer's behavior and actions

D. Insights to better the process of customer retention

The above factors help in achieving successful conversion rates and in knowing what the customers value the most in a call center offerings.

With the rapid rise in Internet-enabled businesses and complex operational environments, it is imperative to be sensitive to the needs of the online customers. Customer needs and call center responses go hand-in-hand even in the virtual world.

Organizational development is an important process for meeting customer expectations. As organizational development primarily focuses on the improvement of the work environment and organization-wide empowerment, this improvement directly affects the way in which customer problems and requests are handled.

If handled with prudence, these processes guide CSRs to achieve results based on realistic goals and standards.

7.3 Management Support—Customer-Centered Leadership

Inculcating CEM and CRM in a call center is a big organizational change. For any organizational change to become effective, leadership is vital. CEM and CRM need to be an explicit component of the business agenda. Leaders need to use their reach and power 'top-down' to transform CEM and CRM from mere functional areas to strategic goals, only then call centers get to experience true payoff from customer experience and relationship management efforts.

The leadership team needs to follow through this journey of transformation by ensuring that their organization understands the rationale of the change, and this is achieved through their own actions and decisions—leaders need to act as role models; the customer-centric culture that starts at the top tier of a call center.

The executive component needs to put in place procedures related to the following aspects:

A. Leadership must ensure that the customers are a part of all that a call center does, right from the corporate mindset to working policies and procedures.

B. Provide and promote the necessary tools and provisions needed to have a high-class quality assurance program in place.

C. Introduce a provision where lessons from the past are recorded and analyzed. Conduct training sessions to share the lessons learned so that CSRs leverage and apply these corporate learnings to new situations.

D. Provide full management buy-in in establishing proper reporting measures on all facets of customer management.

E. Executive support for better people management is an absolute. Leaders need to provide facilities that create an engaging workplace. Research figures suggest that being able to engage with a real person in a collaborative environment is one of the most important drivers of customer satisfaction. CSRs need management backing to provide effective real-time services. Only then CSRs are able to engage their customers in the co-creation of mutual value.

F. Emphasize that knowledge reserves can never go waste. Provide the necessary environment where employees get to learn more about customer relationships.

G. Top management needs to provide all the resources and infrastructure to their staff for creating the required level of brand awareness, brand association and brand loyalty. Management needs to establish a brand name for itself in terms of thought leadership, which then needs to flow into each and every employee and finally get reflected in customer experiences and relationships.

Only when the top executives make decisions consistent with the CEM and CRM strategy and exhibit top-level accountability, CSRs will be able to achieve the 90/10 Excellent Service Rule, i.e., 90 percent of the customer's experience is controllable and only 10 percent is uncontrollable.

Spotlight Tip
It is much easier to get time and resources from top management, if CSRs show corporate contribution through call center operations.

7.4 Customer Experience Excellence—Drivers of Loyalty

The drivers of customer loyalty result in a differentiated customer experience and help in transforming a call center into a center of excellence in customer experience management.

They help in adopting the new art and science of customer experience excellence—right from product and service focus to customer focus and then shifting from customer focus to customer experience excellence. Let us have a look at these drivers of loyalty:

A. Organization-wide empowerment is necessary for the culture of customer experience and relationship management to become a part of the corporate DNA.

B. Empowering the customers is the next step. Organizations can take the current level of customer engagement to a whole new level by creating customer support groups and communities that have equal, 24/7 access to the knowledge resources that CSRs use to perform their jobs, and the customers should be able to contribute content to these knowledge resources too. This anytime access, increased integration and constant collaboration help the customers to address their problems and requests at a much faster rate thereby enabling the customers to co-create their experiences too.

C. To provide a personalized, immersive, consistent, memorable experience across an array of channels and to generate value from customer relationships, robust business intelligence and analytics tools are needed to capture and monitor customer intelligence at the time of the interaction to detect new patterns and to adapt to shifts. This real-time capturing and monitoring of business intelligence are necessary for call centers to align themselves to their media-savvy customers; it is necessary for answering the question—what do the customers want and how do they want it from you? A combination of predictive and behavioral analysis is needed to identify the key drivers behind customer behavioral patterns and trends.

D. Constant innovation of methods and strategies to adapt to new channels and touch points of interaction is a must to improve customer engagement levels.

E. Organizations need to be a part of the social landscape to capture a larger portion of the customer mindshare than their competitors. For this to happen, they need to engage in a two-way dialog with the customers, and this dialog must start long before a transaction occurs and should continue long after the transaction too.

F. Organizations gain valuable customer experience insights by stepping into their customers' shoes.

G. Content management systems need to be upgraded in order to shift from using content to design simple event-oriented marketing initiatives to developing a strategic solution mindset. These systems need to shift their content focus from product-centric to customer-centric.

H. Cross-pollination of these drivers between other organizational departments should occur too. Cross-pollination leads to the creation of collective ownership of customer experiences and the establishment of an

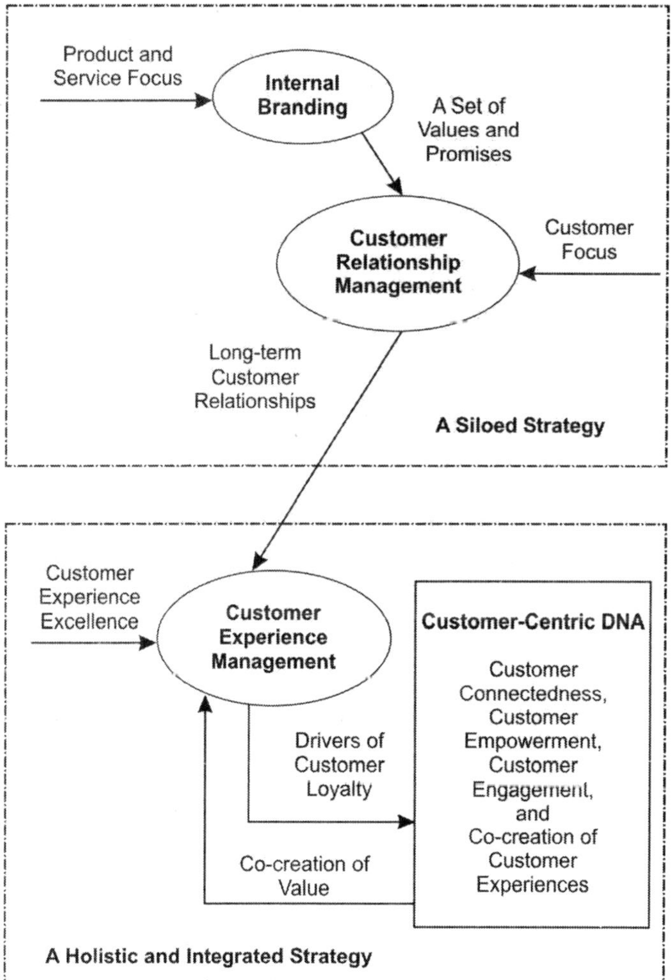

Figure 7.2: Customer Centricity and Experience Maturity

organization-wide model of customer experience delivery. A call center's customers' positive experiences and their subsequent loyalty are its biggest brand, and cross-pollination increases the value of this brand.

Spotlight Tip
An organization's brand promises and values are only as rich and unique as the customer experience itself.

Customer experience excellence is an organizational mindset. It is not something an organization is born with; it is something that an organization becomes. Customer centricity and experience maturity occur when call centers shift their focus from internal branding to customer relationship management, and finally from customer relationships to customer experiences in order to optimize the entire customer journey.

8 Performance—Ringing Up Big Numbers

Measuring call center performance has attracted much attention and investment in the recent years. Performance measurement and management is about evaluating the capacity of the workforce to influence the bottom line. Call center performance is not merely about providing 24 hours a day, 7 days a week service; it goes beyond this. Call center performance revolves around creating quality-driven processes and models that close the gaps and keep a call center way ahead of the competition. It is about building service around the customers by providing on-going monitoring of call processing, tracking and managing.

What is the purpose of performance management, quality monitoring and benchmarking, and what areas a call center needs to benchmark in order to institutionalize best-in-breed business practices are discussed in this chapter.

8.1 Performance Management Model—A Zero-Complaint Environment

Customer satisfaction has moved to the forefront of call center performance goals. The need to provide *quality* care is certainly not a new issue, but this aspect has become very critical today as the customers wield a great influence and expect a lot more; this is where performance management models step in.

Spotlight Tip
Provide line-of-sight visibility to the customers by aligning their expectations to organization performance goals.

Performance management models are systems that provide real-time critical performance data and forecast trends and statistics to improve various performance aspects and the service delivery of call centers. Their main aim is to create a *Zero-Complaint Environment*. It is an environment that has zero tolerance for complaints. 80 percent of the customers who call with a complaint purchase from an organization again only if their complaints are properly handled, and this is where performance management plays a big role. Tools like Balanced Scorecards and Dashboards are often used to measure performance in an objective manner. These real-time tools also help CSRs to manage their own performance, which is a great motivation to perform better in itself. A Dashboard is a comprehensive ready-to-use tool used for managing and measuring call center performance. It provides a visual interface in the form of charts, graphs, etc., for monitoring performance indicators. A Balanced Scorecard goes one step further. It is not just a performance measurement tool, but also a strategic performance management tool that provides a more 'balanced' view of performance against strategic targets. It considers both financial and non-financial factors in determining the performance levels.

The business objective is the key factor in developing the perfect performance model. There are several objectives like high returns, high customer satisfaction levels, consistent customer experiences or new markets. This high-level objective helps to establish performance goals for both individuals and the entire organization.

As there is performance data coming in from various tools, sources and systems, the performance model needs to take care of integrating these inputs into one unified, comprehensible format. And this is necessary to align call center Key Performance Indicators (KPI) and corporate goals. A KPI is also known as a Key Success Indicator (KSI). It is a quantifiable measure that generally consists of a timeframe, a target and a benchmark.

PQS = Productivity, Quality and Service are the most critical factors of call center performance management. KPIs and best practices help to keep track of the PQS aspects; they are the backbone of any call center performance management model. They also help in determining whether a particular call center qualifies for call center certification or not.

Cost-effective IT models and strategic investment in technologies like customer information management, IVR systems, etc., help to boost the performance level and savings.

Another measurable factor that is growing in importance is Corporate Social Responsibility. Being "premier corporate citizens" is the *mantra* for improving the quality of service extended to a call center's major stakeholders—Customers. The customers are not only interested in the quality of products and services, but they are also affected favorably when organizations have a positive impact on the society and the environment. It is about integrating economic, social and environmental concerns with the business that call centers do with their customers; this goes to show that such call centers want to operate in a socially responsible and ethical manner.

Employees are another key indicator to test the performance health of call centers. Comparison of the employees' performance with competition and industry standards is a good way of putting things in perspective. A holistic people management system is a must for a workable performance management model, as a highly engaged workforce drives the business performance.

Measuring effectiveness and quality (Qualitative measures) is just as important as measuring efficiency and quantity (Quantitative measures). Qualitative measures are textual in nature (such as very satisfied, not satisfied and moderately satisfied) and they are based on subjective interpretation either from a customer's or CSR's perspective. Quantitative measures are numerical in nature (such as on a rating scale of 0-10) and they are derived by adding, counting or averaging numbers. Both these measures are necessary to measure customer service and CSR productivity; one without the other results in an inaccurate performance measurement. All this while organizations had been spending too much time and money on measurements that are focused on volume, but with the increasing emphasis on customer experiences, they have now also started to include qualitative measurements like customer satisfaction and customer lifetime value in the corporate agenda. Quantitative measures are about "how fast", whereas "how well" is measured by qualitative measures, for example how fast are calls being answered and how well are calls being answered; not only the number of seconds a call lasts, but also the value of each and every call is important.

All performance metrics should be defined using the FABRIC formula—Focused, Appropriate, Balanced, Robust, Integrated and Cost-effective.

Having CSRs handle calls within 20 seconds is good, but if there is no proper performance management model that helps CSRs to recognize opportunities for an additional sale or repeat business, then their actions are unproductive. To ensure that all these aspects are handled properly, we need to have four main components in place to bring about a successful performance management model:

A. Performance Goals: These are goals that will be measured during the review period. They reflect the critical success factors that need to be met in order to achieve peak performance. Both the top management and CSRs need to give their inputs in defining these goals. Buy-in from all stakeholders is necessary for proper tracking purposes. Goals should be defined using the SMART rule—Specific, Measurable, Attainable, Relevant and Timely.

B. Reviews and Follow-up: Performance reviews are conducted by managers and supervisors to assign ratings to their CSRs. A rating is assigned for each performance indicator based on the comparison between the performance expectation and the CSR's actual performance. Based on this evaluation, new performance goals and remedial measures are designed. Follow-up is necessary for CSRs to know how well they are doing in comparison to their goals. Follow-up is necessary for aligning supporting elements of CSR's performance in terms of rewards and recognition.

C. Constant Feedback: Timely and objective feedback sessions are required to ensure that star performers are identified and rewarded so that they continue to perform well, prove to be role models for others and rise above the performance baseline. At the same time, constant feedback also helps in pinpointing underperformers so that appropriate reorientation strategies can be designed to bring them back on the performance baseline.

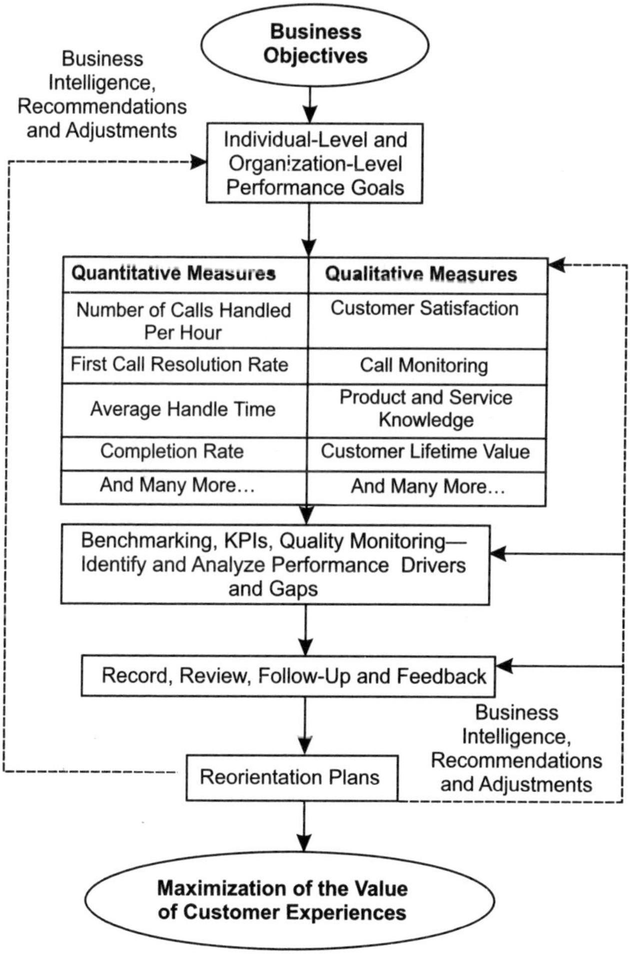

Figure 8.1: The Performance Management Model

D. Reorientation: Reorientation through continuous coaching, process adjustments, improvement plans, training, rewarding top performance and motivation is needed to fill the gaps in the processes of individual-level and organization-level goals, quantitative and qualitative measures, benchmarking standards, KPIs and quality monitoring, and record, review, follow-up and feedback. This process is iterative in nature. It loops through these processes more than once. This iteration is necessary to fine-tune the performance management model and customer experience value delivery strategies.

These components aid in making fact-based decisions to leap ahead to excellence. They provide an objective basis for evaluating how well call centers are meeting the expectations and needs of their customers.

Call centers need to reassess and revise their performance operating procedures and models from time to time in order to attain holistic performance maturity, right from the definition of performance goals and measures to the assessment and reorientation plans.

8.1.1 KPI Catalogue—They say You are What You Measure

Choosing the right set of KPIs is the key to measuring the business performance in accurate terms. KPIs guide call centers in aligning their employee goals with their organizational vision and objective, and in ensuring that call center teams are actually doing what they should be doing.

What is the percentage of calls that are attended to within a specific time frame? Is your call center maximizing service while minimizing abandoned calls? What is the best time of the day for CSRs to make sales conversions? What is the percentage of calls that resolve the customer's issues? KPIs help to answer these as well as many more questions. They help to compare performance against competition.

Some of the main KPIs are as follows:

A. Agent Utilization is the most accurate measure of labor efficiency. When agent utilization is high, cost per call is low, and vice versa.

A Word of Caution
If call centers push the agent utilization rate, then turnover rate is going to be high as CSRs will be overburdened and feel that they are being pushed to the limits.

B. First Call Resolution Rate is also called as one contact resolution; this measure tells us how many customers get their requests/complaints resolved on the first call itself. A high rate indicates a high customer satisfaction level. For example, more than 90 percent of inquires resolved on the first call made could be a measurable performance standard.

C. Cost Per Call is the total costs (fixed and variable) divided by the total calls for a given period of time. The more calls your call center handles, the cheaper the cost per call would be.

D. Average Handle Time (AHT) is the sum of Average Talk Time and Average After-Call Work for a specified time period.

E. Average Talk Time (ATT) is defined as the average amount of time spent talking to the customers for each call.

F. Number of abandoned calls is also called a lost call; the caller disconnects the call before reaching a CSR. For example, less than 10 percent of calls abandoned could be a measureable performance standard.

G. Adherence to Schedule is a common metric to measure the degree to which CSRs stick to their schedules.

H. Calls Per Hour is the average number of calls a CSR is able to take per hour.

I. Sales Effectiveness is measured in terms of the percentage of calls/transactions in which a sales opportunity is converted into an actual sale.

J. Cross-sell/Up-sell Revenue

K. Longest Wait Time (LWT) is the longest time a caller has to wait before the call is answered.

L. System availability and utilization in terms of bandwidth, servers, back-up and other equipments.

M. And many more...

Each of the above KPIs is analyzed in terms of its status, trend, actual value, target value, variance and variance percentage.

KPIs which a call center uses vary depending on the type and functions of a call center. For example, a sales-driven call center is more interested in measuring KPIs like Sales Effectiveness and Average Call Length, whereas in a help desk environment, KPIs like Response Time and Call Abandon Rate are relevant.

8.1.2 More Tools—Little Things Make a Big Difference

Comprehensive call center metrics is the key to measuring performance accurately. Apart from these internal metrics and in-house quality monitoring and quality assurance programs, there are several supporting tools to improve the performance levels.

Self-evaluation systems are very beneficial as they encourage CSRs to monitor and manage their own performance. Self-evaluation, in a way, provides a means of empowerment—where there is empowerment there is accountability. Self-evaluation motivates CSRs to introduce changes to improve their involvement in the performance management process.

Are your CSRs performing to the optimum level for each and every call? Are your CSRs successful in closing the sale? This is where "mystery shopping" comes in handy. Mystery shopping is an assessment technique of evaluating how call centers are handling their calls; it gives the call center management an opportunity to assess how well their call center is functioning from the customers' perspective. In this technique, "secret" shoppers call the call center under a false pretense and record and compile various parameters of call center interactions (tone and attitude of a CSR, wait time, service consistency) in the form of unbiased, comprehensive reports. These reports help call center management to identify lost opportunities, to assess the success of training programs, to create accountability, and to identify star performers and underperformers.

De-pulping is an important technique of improving CSRs' productivity. Eradicating messy filing cabinets and replacing them with powerful databases makes tons of information accessible in a few mouse clicks. All customer intelligence, knowledge documents, and anything else that is paper-based and is needed by CSRs to provide quick, effective customer services, if converted to electronic format, saves them a lot of time and cost. This saving takes them closer to the benchmarks. There are software products that reorganize CSRs' desktops to provide them with an intelligent, unified view into all customer interactions and data thereby facilitating centralized performance tracking.

8.2 Benchmarking—Best-in-Class Practices

Definition of Benchmarking: A reference point or standard of excellence against which similar or subsequent marks are compared (Barker, 2003). In other words, benchmarking is the measurement of the quality of best practices in comparison to practices both within an industry and outside it. It pinpoints gaps in performance and provides pointers to fill these gaps too. The key success measures of measuring call center performance entail a gamut of benchmarking standards for various areas, right from the employee recruitment process to training practices and from operations to retention strategies. What helps to set and measure benchmarks are customer satisfaction surveys, regulations, industry benchmarks, Service Level Agreements, team meetings, etc.

Benchmarking was pioneered in the 1970s by the Xerox Corporation and today it is helping business entities across domains in enhancing their bottom line revenues.

Benchmarking is conducted to find best practices. There are two broad categories of benchmarking—process benchmarking and competitive benchmarking. Process benchmarking is about reviewing internal business operations and work procedures and comparing them with industry standards, whereas competitive benchmarking is about comparing an organization's operations, practices and performance measures with that of its competitors with similar function, customer profile and size. It is always good to remember that what seems to be a best practice for one center may not be for the next.

Benchmarking starts by determining which processes and operations to benchmark, followed by identifying the key performance indicators and drivers and selecting competitor benchmark call centers, and then measuring performance of competitors and own performance, and then deriving performance statistics and metrics and pinpointing performance gaps, and finally implementing improvement plans to bring the performance level closer to the baseline.

Service level is another important factor for linking resources and results. The staffing level and the schedules should be based on your service level objective in order to minimize costs, maximize profits, reduce agent burnout, reduce abandoned calls, and above all meet customer needs. There is no set industry standard for the service level target but many call centers follow the *80/20 principle*—80 percent calls answered in 20 seconds. Other methods to arrive at the service level target are by following competition, tracking similar organizations and soliciting inputs from customer surveys.

A Word of Caution
Having a high service level is not the main point but achieving it on a constant basis is crucial.

Profiling employees based on Emotional Intelligence assessments is an important method of benchmarking call center performance. ACD statistics are also a key source for deriving benchmarking-related data.

There are several techniques of performing benchmarking. Rigorous industry comparison and analysis can be performed by commissioning research to a research provider firm. Other techniques include conferences, commercial databases, forums, peer group data, reports, research papers and studies on best practices.

Table 8.1: Benchmarking Areas

Leadership	Operations
Workforce Management	Front-line Training Practices
Communication	Call Quality
Planning Tools	Customer Experience
Adherence to Protocols	Cost-Efficiency
Reward and Recognition	Data Collection and Usage
Speed of Service	Call Resolution
Technology	Customer Satisfaction
Customer Research	Measurement Techniques
CSR Satisfaction	Accessibility
Attrition Rate	Schedule Efficiency
Resource Utilization	And many more...

Benchmarks used by all types of call centers focus on the following areas:

A. Compare a call center's performance with the performance of others.

B. Compare performance of team members.

C. Identify strengths and weaknesses.

D. Identify new areas of improvement.

E. Develop a time-phased action plan for remedying variances.

F. Identify industry trends and competitor developments.

All the above benchmarking factors help in identifying "customer-facing stars". Best practices and standards are constantly evolving. Therefore, it is important for call centers to continually update their benchmarking standards in order to enjoy competitive success.

8.3 Quality Monitoring—Recording and Beyond

The processes of recording and analyzing customer communications across channels, and then using insights from these processes to improve customer experiences form the heart of the Quality Monitoring System (QMS) in call centers.

In large call centers, a dedicated team for quality monitoring is a great option, whereas in smaller call centers, CSRs' direct supervisors or team leaders perform this function.

QMS can be a successful corporate initiative only when each and every stakeholder is convinced of the fact that it is going to be beneficial to them; their goals and needs and the reasons behind adopting various techniques for quality monitoring should resonate with each other.

Management needs to ensure that their employees have a say in managing their own performance. QMS is not about rebuking weak performers, but it is a team effort geared towards exceeding quality goals. CSRs need to be made aware of the fact that they are a significant component of quality programs. Only then they demonstrate the willingness to assume responsibility and ownership of their performance successes and failures.

Techniques like walk around observation, auditing, record and review, call recording, screen recording and silent monitoring create visible accountability for the PQS factors of call center performance management.

8.3.1 Techniques—Observe, Record, Review, Retrieve and Improve

Walk around observation is a proactive and engaging method of ongoing coaching as supervisors and managers can impart personalized coaching and mentoring to their CSRs in solving real problems on the job. Supervisors and managers need to be in constant touch with their teams through live monitoring and observation. Appreciating on-the-spot CSR performance is a great way of convincing CSRs that this technique is not about snooping but about collaborative teamwork.

Audits are the best way of performing a SWOT Analysis (SWOT stands for strengths, weaknesses, opportunities and threats) of call center operations. Gap identification, risk identification and status reporting of core operational areas are some of their main functions. They also help in analyzing the quality of interactions. Audits facilitate call centers to reduce call waiting times. They provide valuable inputs to the management review process thereby ensuring that senior managers are fully aware of all quality-related dimensions; senior managers use these inputs to identify action items and design remedial measures.

In Call Recording and Monitoring, call centers record and index calls, monitor conversations, and retrieve reports based on recorded calls between callers and CSRs. Now with latest technologies, recording and retrieval is possible in real-time and they also support hybrid environments like Web-based Chat Transcripts, Mobile, etc. Advanced features like remote monitoring, automatic, manual and voice activated recording, and complex search facilities for call recording retrieval are some of the advantages of modern setups. Quality monitoring specialists, trainers and supervisors use this technique to increase customer satisfaction, monitor agent performance, verify accuracy of information and reduce liability. They are also able to confirm whether or not CSRs meet compliance requirements. This technique ensures fair sampling and unbiased review by monitoring and recording each CSR at different times of the day. It is also useful in recording calls which come from high-value customers.

In Screen Recording, call centers capture agent desktop activity thereby enabling supervisors and managers to literally see how their CSRs are handling each call. By playing back screen recordings along with voice recordings, supervisors and managers evaluate the correlation between a CSR's performance and assessment results.

In Silent Monitoring, managers and supervisors silently listen and monitor in-progress calls without the knowledge of CSRs and callers. The main purpose of this technique is to measure performance indicators like AHT and Call-backs, rate CSR abilities in terms of communication confidence, voice tone, etiquettes, calmness, knowledge competence and empathy, determine whether or not CSRs comply with best practices and policies, and identify employee development and training opportunities.

All these techniques enhance the QMS as they help in identifying shortcomings in the workflow, prioritizing critical opportunities, pinpointing sound processes and unearthing the best practices by providing just-in-time business intelligence.

8.4 Customer Satisfaction Survey—They are the Best Judge

How do we find out whether your customers are satisfied? The best way to find out whether your customers are satisfied is through the customer satisfaction survey; the following worksheet aids you in this. A completed survey form is a gold mine of information. According to research studies, in a competitive environment, an organization with "high customer satisfaction" can charge up to 10 percent premium for similar products and services than its competitors. In other words, it takes 10 percent price differential for a "Very Satisfied" customer to consider switching to another organization.

This survey helps to understand the customer base better, measure call center performance and provide insights about sales trends. It also helps to focus limited resources on the really important aspects of providing first rate customer experiences.

Customer Name:

Please answer the following using options Yes or No:

A. Is this the first time you have contacted us?

B. If not the first time, how do you usually contact our call center? (Tick all that apply)

Telephone

Fax

E-Mail

Web

Chat

Others

C. Will you recommend us to your friends, colleagues and relatives?

Please rate the following aspects on a scale of 1-5, 1 being Not At All and 5 being Very Satisfied. You can also include any comments and observations along with your ratings.

CSR Competency	Rating
How happy are you with the way your calls were answered by the CSR in terms of time, service, undivided attention and information?	
How well do you think the CSR handled your call in terms of attitude, courtesy, language skills, flow of conversation, empathy, professionalism and listening comprehension?	

(Contd...)

How satisfied do you feel about the CSR's awareness of your business needs and responsiveness to your requests and questions?	
Quality of Service	**Rating**
Are the service levels being met?	
Is the implementation of new features and enhancements in the products/services hassle-free?	
Do the products/services delivered perform as specified?	
Effectiveness Indicators (cost, delivery, etc.)	**Rating**
How satisfied do you feel about the timeliness of the product/service delivery?	
How satisfied are you with the value delivered at the end of the transaction?	

Please rate the following on a scale of 1-5. 1 indicates lowest and 5 indicates highest.

A. Product/Service Quality

B. Product/Service Benefits

C. Product/Service Reliability and Consistency

Overall satisfaction rating:

1: Very Dissatisfied

2: Somewhat Satisfied

3: Neither Satisfied Nor Dissatisfied

4: Somewhat Satisfied

5: Very Satisfied

If you have any additional comments about how we can improve our services, please fill them in here:

May we contact you about any of your responses?

Contact Details (Optional):

8.5 Performance Parameters—Reach the Peak

The following is a checklist of the performance parameters needed to achieve peak performance in call centers:

A. Quality Assurance: Proactive attitude towards problems and gaps in service quality. A real-time quality assurance system is needed to identify problems and gaps as they occur. The system should easily adapt to business changes in order to anticipate new problems and gaps long before they surface and escalate.

B. Business Relationships: Happy customers are a call center's most precious asset. Requests resolved, queries answered, confidentiality in terms of customer lists and intelligence maintained, and polite service received, all result in happy customers.

C. Communication: Too much data and information overload on CSRs causes miscommunication. If all the data and information are stored in a centralized database, then access becomes a lot easier. Electronic storage ensures a smooth communication cycle without relying on a single point or a manual source.

D. Reporting: Organized, regular reporting based on historical analysis and real-time data is an absolute must. What gets measured gets done; hence useful, timely and relevant reports are needed to implement the improving-in-the-moment principle. Timely reporting helps in converting negative customer experiences into positive ones.

E. Call Monitoring and Evaluation: A digital recording system with sophisticated software is a great way of focusing on various call-related quality factors.

Communication at Various Levels—From Acquistion to Loyalty

9

Call centers are real-time entities; they are about leveraging real-time communication to create webs of association. In today's volatile market conditions, effective communication at various levels helps to transform your call center into a proactive, real-time enterprise. A CSR typically communicates with more customers in a week than most employees interact in their entire career.

The main function of call center communication is enabling the journey from customer acquisition to customer loyalty by humanizing the hub of interaction. It is about creating a highly engaging environment—where everyone wins!

The key to effective communication at various levels is awareness and knowledge. Aspects like 'active' listening and paraphrasing help to avoid communication glitches and develop intercultural sensitivity. They also may increase repurchase intention even if the request/problem is not resolved.

Terms like Emotional Intelligence (EI) and Cross-cultural communication are in vogue. They instill a positive perspective in all the stakeholders involved in the communication process. They help to build energy inducing emotions, which are needed to dissolve problems in all communication scenarios.

This chapter discusses communication-related topics to help you understand how the focus of customer relationship management in call centers has shifted from products and services to the customers and the customer experiences. It is about providing customized services at the speed of light and enhancing customer-facing operations like marketing, support and sales.

9.1 Connecting with the Customers—Think Before You Talk

According to industry statistics, 86 percent customers quit doing business with organizations because of a bad customer experience. In an era of customer empowerment, connecting with the customers is critical for the business world. No software or hardware can empathize with the customers, only people can.

Connecting with the customers is about understanding both the substance and the manner of what they are communicating with you. Asking the right set of questions helps to get what you want. It leads to an honest, respectful communication, and more than that it leads to meeting the customer needs and expectations. This area is another crucial factor of a knowledge worker. As a knowledge worker, call center communication is yet another medium for you to create new knowledge reserves and transfer them to your fellow workers.

Customer communication is a major source of untapped revenue streams. Organizations of today have become aware of the value of mining data embedded within this communication across channels in order to use it to serve their customers in a better way.

Research has proved that customer issues see resolution only 45 percent of the time when handled by CSRs with poor communication abilities. To move forward, organizations need to "reinvent the wheel". Instead of following vague business phrases, use simple and clear language to get your message across.

Certain call center customer communication situations are more sensitive in nature, for example, dealing with customer issues like death, accident or depression. CSRs working in such call centers need to always take care of the 'human element' first and then focus on maximizing sales. In short, CSRs have to have the right mix of interpersonal touch and business sense.

Spotlight Tip
Use the best leading questions to obtain the desired information from the customers. Do not use internal corporate jargon as the customers may not be able to understand the same. Always reinforce positive interactions with the customers.

Web-enabled communication with the customers is on the rise. Automatic response systems catering to customer e-mails are slowly and steadily becoming widespread. Even in these automated scenarios, organizations need to put careful thought while designing them. They need to add the personal touch that will keep the customers coming back to them. Rewrite templates and auto responses to cater to the customer requests in precise and clear terms. Simple components of the automated systems like Auto Greetings need to be designed with extreme care. They are prerecorded greeting messages that play automatically when a customer calls. Even delay announcements need to be worded properly in order to encourage the callers to wait for a CSR to become free.

Each customer interacts and behaves differently. A successful CSR is one who relates to and handles these customer dynamics and diversity with panache. Live chat support in the form of forums, telephone, social networking or chat adds that personal touch to digitized communication. Another advantage of a live chat scenario is that CSRs handle multiple communication links simultaneously.

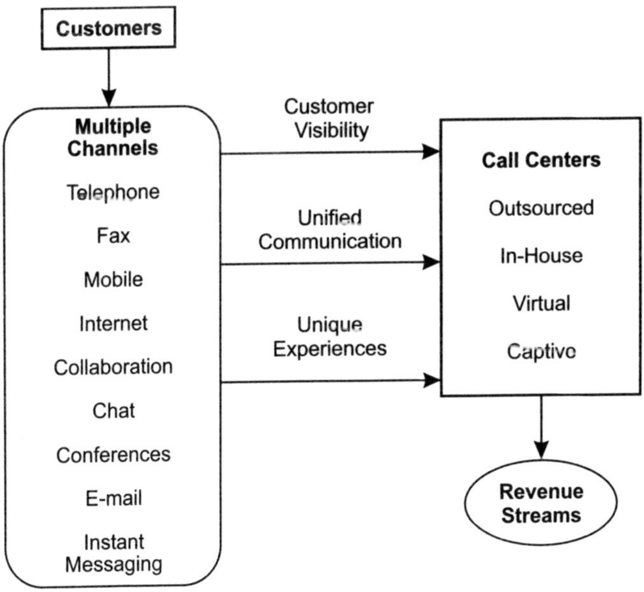

Figure 9.1: The Customer Communication Channels and Revenue Streams

Call centers must strive hard to provide a unified communication delivery model across all customer touch points in order to cater to all aspects of communication in real-time and create unique experiences. This in turn ensures that call centers act as a profit arm of their organizations.

9.1.1 Cross-Cultural Communication—Long-Lasting Contacts

Most of the call center players belong to a multi-ethnic background. Cross-cultural communication plays a key role in developing interpersonal skills. Giving importance to your customers' cultural background and what they have to say goes a long way in building long-lasting business contacts. Cross-cultural communication is a way of dealing with diverse communication contexts by combining the plus points of various cultural perspectives.

Connecting with the outside world is about cross-cultural communication. Culture takes many forms and one of them is verbal and non-verbal communication, which is a critical component of the call center communication cycle; more than 60 percent of communication is non-verbal. Call centers have to constantly revisit and revise their approach and strategies to improve cross-cultural communication. The following objectives need to be met in order to manage customer relationships properly and to ensure that the customers feel they are more than an account number:

A. Cross-cultural communication needs a thorough understanding of one's own cultural background.

B. Understanding values and expectations belonging to the culture of the target customer.

C. Applying this understanding to the customer's behavior and his personal space, beliefs, language, accent, level of openness, etc.

D. Conducting a cross-cultural awareness training to learn and maintain etiquettes.

E. Developing methods of managing customer relationships.

F. Developing personal strategies and techniques for managing cultural shocks.

Once these factors are in place, call center employees are in a position to adjust their behaviors accordingly and prepare their sales pitches effectively. Once these objectives are achieved, the answers to questions like 'Are your responses in sync with the words and the meanings behind the words you have chosen?', 'Are you able to create common interests and goals with the customer through effective verbal and non-verbal communication?', etc., become easy to find.

Apart from in-house training, call centers need to bring in training content and delivery by outside experts and specialists.

Within a call center there need to be systems and applications that help CSRs to translate insights from customer communication into business opportunities. There need to be well-planned interfaces for sharing communication-related data between call centers and their departmental counterparts like sales, data warehouse, marketing, etc., so that well-rounded decisions are made.

Spotlight Tip
Cross-cultural communication is not only about communication. It involves other branches like human psychology, thought processing, anthropology, marketing theories and cultural studies too. Knowledge of these aspects = A Great CSR.

Time is also considered as a cultural factor. In the west, time is money; it is considered crucial in achieving success. In the east, it is more to do with the natural phenomenon of time elapsing between the origin and end of the world. All these time-related aspects need to be kept in mind, especially in conflict resolution and negotiation scenarios.

Humor is also an important part of the cultural fabric. Humor is very difficult to export across boundaries. As a CSR, one needs to be wary of the importance level of humor in the target culture. As far as possible avoid using too many colloquial expressions. Humor based on religion, ethnicity, color and caste is a sure-fire way of putting off the customers.

As call centers are technology-driven units, the attitude towards technology and its usage plays a crucial role in cross-cultural communication. Certain cultures view technology as a means of running and controlling each and every aspect of life, certain cultures view technology with skepticism and there are others who feel that technology and life can co-exist harmoniously. The attitude towards the technological tools and resources needs to be kept in sight while dealing with people. For example, if you are communicating with the customers from the east, you need to be aware of the fact that they operate in a business environment where they consider technology as something that can be controlled.

9.2 Emotional Intelligence—Respond, Not React

Emotional Intelligence (EI) is about developing personal and social capacity to build trust and mutual respect. The main traits of an EI-driven performer are explained in the following paragraphs.

Data and information can be transmitted through electronic means, but true knowledge in terms of experiences, insights, rapport, trust and diverse perspectives can be acquired through emotional intelligence. Recently, findings of psychologists have shown that a 1 percent improvement in emotional climate and trust-building leads to a 2 percent increase in revenues. An agent who is in tune with his or her own emotions and mood is much more likely to be able to understand and empathize with the customers' emotions and moods.

EI should exist not only for the external stakeholders—customers, but also for internal customers—sales, marketing and service departments. Emotionally Intelligent Communication across all levels in a call center is the need of the hour.

Nowadays, most call centers conduct popular Emotional Intelligence Quotient (EQ) assessments like the Multifactor Emotional Intelligence Scale or the Seligman Attributional Style Questionnaire on prospective employees. The main focus of such assessments is to differentiate between average and high-performing human capital based on various emotional competencies. Results from such tests also guide call centers in developing programs to enhance their employees' thinking and actions. It is proven that people with a high Emotional Quotient

(EQ) perform better in the workplace as compared to people who have a low EQ and a reasonably good IQ.

Managers and supervisors need to lead by example in order to imbibe the EQ culture. They need to act as emotional mentors and model the appropriate behavioral patterns through their words and actions. They need to treat each agent as a unique personality and convince their teams that they are accessible and ready to help agents in all work-related matters. This model behavior motivates agents to treat their customers in a similar manner. Managers and supervisors need to work out tips and techniques to help their employees reconfigure their emotional landscape in such a way that it becomes appropriate for any given customer-specific situation.

As has been stated earlier, call centers are more than just answering calls; they are about catering to the needs of the customers. Emotional Intelligence is about building a "learning communication context", where people involved are more aware of and in control of their emotions. Only when CSRs learn to self-manage, self-control their emotional highs and lows, they are able to develop awareness of and manage well the customers' emotional needs. This is necessary as emotions and moods are contagious, and one disgruntled CSR can quickly affect the entire team.

The role of the executive wing in the process of developing EQ is crucial. They need to model 'the feeling of connection', only then CSRs follow in their footsteps. Without that feeling of connection, the customers will go elsewhere.

Self-awareness is the most important skill needed to build workplace emotional intelligence and to understand what is going on inside the customer's mind. Self-reflection is one such key technique that helps CSRs to improve their self-awareness level. Self-reflection helps CSRs to reorient behavioral patterns. It helps them to develop and nourish behavioral patterns that increase work productivity and achieve work goals in unison. Self-reflection and self-analysis is done by seeking answers to questions like:

A. Do I stay composed under work pressures?

B. Do I decipher the customer's emotions correctly?
C. Do I jump to conclusions?
D. Do I communicate with the customers with full honesty?
E. Am I aware of how my behavior affects my team and customers?
F. Am I able to segregate the positive emotional triggers from the negative ones?
G. Am I able to take feedback in a positive sense?
H. Am I able to identify how my feelings and emotions affect my performance?
I. Am I able to handle irate customers?

Once CSRs have answers to these questions, they are able to self-control, self-manage and self-adapt to difficult customer situations. They are able to stay calm and positive even under pressure. Self-awareness helps them to not only tune into their own feelings and emotions, but also tune into the feelings and emotions of others—their customers. This sense of empathy helps call centers to establish corporate-level social awareness, which adds to each and every team's emotional level. The key benefit of this whole process is to anticipate and respond to customer needs in sync with the customer's emotional cues. Over a period of time, this synchronization facilitates top management, managers, supervisors and CSRs to discern the nuances of the customers' emotional landscape, handle difficult customer situations with tact, identify potential emotional-level customer-related conflicts, and build a network of positive communications and human energy with the customers.

Rigorous research shows that EQ amounts to a larger percent of successes in leadership and workplace effectiveness as opposed to IQ. Not surprisingly, call centers want to retain leaders, managers, supervisors and CSRs who possess a reasonably high EQ; who are smart with their emotions.

9.3 Maturity—Determine whether Ahead or Behind

Customer satisfaction and monitoring customer satisfaction in a meaningful way is the key to measuring call center maturity. The EI dynamics play a critical role in accelerating a call center's maturity. Performance in areas like corporate culture, work schedules, people, technology, process improvement, services supported, etc., finally gets translated to customer satisfaction. Performance in these areas is improved based on the communications occurring at various levels and among various key players within a call center using the EI dynamics.

The following points help you assess and determine whether your call center is ahead or behind on the maturity curve. Some of these points have been discussed in detail elsewhere in this book while the rest are right here in this chapter:

A. Customer Interactions: Interaction-handling processes have to be flawless and they need to promote well-managed relationships. Call centers that have the capacity to seamlessly integrate customer interaction data through intelligent desktop applications perform better and faster. Such smart desktops enable CSRs to navigate a labyrinth of applications easily and also the need for duplicate data entry is eliminated. This ensures that CSRs spend quality time on handling customer interactions rather than wasting time on navigating through complex menus and multiple applications.

B. Skills-based Routing: It is an advanced form of call routing where the calls are filtered and directed to CSRs with the most appropriate skills and experience levels required by the call. Call centers that match CSR skills with the customer profile and the type of call perform the best. With an expanding customer base, merely matching the skills with the prior call patterns won't help.

C. Self-service Options: Call centers that handle regular queries and common issues by deploying web-based self-service applications allow the customers to perform tasks by themselves.

D. Multiple Channels: The customers have become more demanding and use various channels of communication. Call centers that offer their services through the channel of their customers' choice definitely top the competition.

E. Data Capture and Analysis: Call centers that have the capabilities to extract and analyze data from multiple sources score one more point on the maturity curve. Tools and procedures for capturing customer inputs and responses need to be in place. You cannot achieve maturity, if you are not listening to your customers and addressing the issues they tell you are the most important.

F. Accurate Metrics: Call centers that have adopted new metrics like profit per call, referral rate and cross-sell rate, rather than just sticking to the traditional AHT are doing better business.

G. Virtualization: Building on the virtual service offerings through various options like work-at-home agents or telecommuting employees adds a new dimension to the maturity level. Virtual setups help call centers to take advantage of emerging trends and get that much needed maturity edge over the others.

H. Performance Optimization Strategies: Collaboration between other departments (like marketing, training, human resources and finance) and the call center unit in terms of intelligence sharing helps to build holistic approaches towards customer satisfaction. By dynamically sharing data and by knocking down walls across departments, call centers are able to gain a 360 degree view of the customer's needs and behaviors; hence more mature solutions.

10 Tools of the Trade—The Newest and the Coolest

Let me cite a hypothetical example (but it does happen to a lot of us in real life as well) to bring out the importance of selecting the right mix of technologies for call centers. When I checked the status of my order for the new digital camera that I wanted to send as a gift to my mother, I was told my order had been canceled. But in reality, there was a computer glitch and the software had reported the incorrect order status. If not properly selected, configured and integrated to suit your call center needs, tools and technologies play havoc.

CSRs use computers, telephones and other technology products extensively in their work. The spread of modern technology and computer-enabled tools has radically changed the way customer calls are handled. The modern facilities and the deepening technological penetration have helped in maximizing the service throughput thereby fully utilizing the human resources. Technology is an important factor in managing customer experiences. Organizations where the customer base runs into a large number, have established dedicated departments that leverage the power of technology to manage customer experiences.

The greatest technology cannot replace efficient employees, but it definitely adds to their productivity level manifold. The main aim of technology-driven call centers is to support real-time transactions, which in turn help to reduce time delays, minimize rework and cut down costs. The right choice of technologies affects the performance baseline. Validating and doing an analysis of technologies and products implemented on a regular basis is crucial in call center solutions.

The technology needs and requirements for the various kinds of call centers differ significantly from one another, but there are certain typical technology elements that are needed to get you going. Whether your call center is a large set-up or a micro-center, or whether your call center is outsourced or an in-house facility, there are different types of technological tools needed to run it. In this chapter we deal with the various call center technology components.

Starting Point: Determining the type of call center you have helps you to determine the types of technological products and setups you need.

10.1 The Basic Components—Basic yet Powerful

A typical call center is housed in a wide open space and contains rows after rows of cubicles that emanate a constant buzz of activity. Each cubicle houses a computer for each CSR. Each computer has a telephone set and a headset, which are connected to the outside world through circuits and trunks via a telephone exchange or a point-of-presence facility.

Most large call centers use their own PBX network to handle calls. PBX stands for private branch exchange; an organization's own exclusive in-house telephone exchange to handle both calls made between organization's phones and external calls.

Automatic Call Distributor (ACD) is responsible for routing the customer calls to the appropriate CSRs. Often ACD routes calls based on inputs from the Interactive Voice Response (IVR) system and its own predefined parameters. IVR is normally linked to a database, which it uses to provide automated responses to basic queries. This flow is a typical case of inbound scenario.

In outbound calling, a Predictive Dialer system is also involved. It dials batches of phone numbers in a smart fashion by dialing only those numbers that will get answered by a live person.

With so much of data coming in and going out of the call center, we need a central repository to store it. This is where a database system steps in. Merely storing the data won't do any wonders, what is needed is accurate reporting of the same. A powerful Reporting system gives timely insights into the call center performance.

ACD, IVR, Predictive Dialers, Databases and Reporting Packages, apart from these basics technological components, there are other technological products used for various purposes.

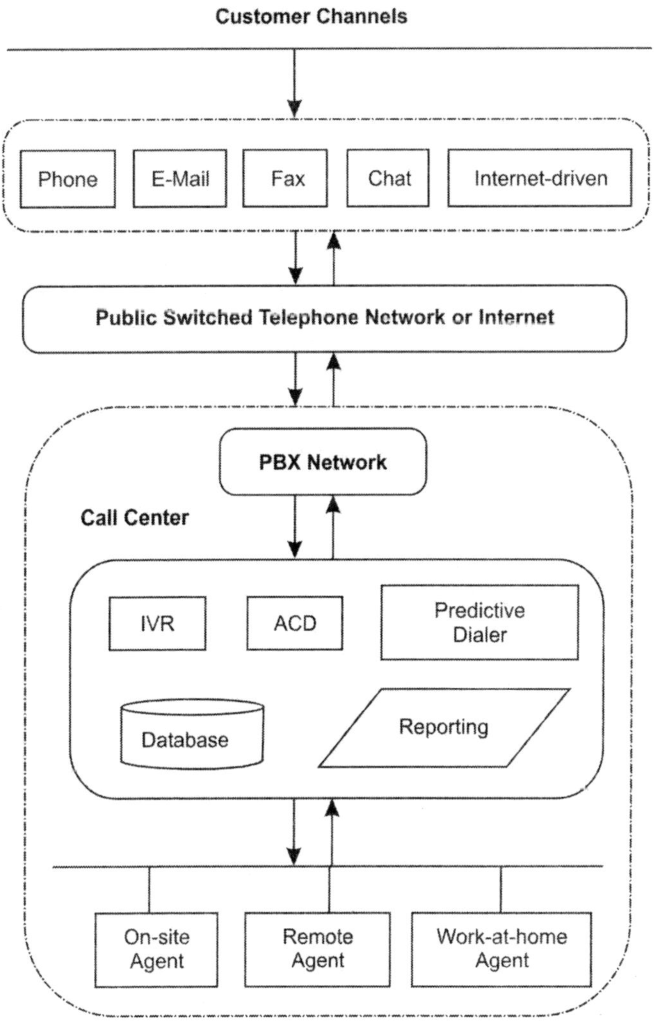

Figure 10.1: The Basic Components

Some of them are E-Mail Management, Customer Relationship Management System, Knowledge Management System, Workforce Management Software, Call Recording Software and Speech Analytics.

Call centers need to configure and integrate these technological tools to handle outages as well. Outages are both technical (heavy call volume, seasonal traffic) and non-technical (natural calamities) in nature. In all cases, call centers need to have proper technology in place to scale up to such situations; the customers must be able to have access to your system under all circumstances.

Spotlight Tip
Perform reality checks 3 months and 12 months after implementing any new application or technology to ensure that they are performing as per the specifications and generating real value in terms of cost savings.

10.2 Automatic Call Distributor—Intelligent Routing

The main aim of Automatic Call Distributor (ACD) is to optimize the distribution of incoming calls so that the callers receive prompt service and the burden of handling calls is distributed evenly among CSRs. Today's ACDs do much more than call routing; they provide advanced features like silent observation, call blending and digital recording.

ACD is the key system that routes incoming calls to specific types of agents based on the call type and its characteristics. This routing is managed based on a database of handling instructions and business rules. Advanced ACD can also pick and choose the most appropriate agent for a particular caller thereby providing a personalized customer experience. ACDs often provide some form of Automatic Number Identification (ANI); ANI is a feature that provides the receiver of the call with the number of the calling phone. This number is used to find further information of the caller from a database system.

ACD plays a vital role during peak hours when CSRs are not available. ACD can queue calls or have a voice mail option in place or play a recorded announcement.

ACD uses call control variables, which are a set of criteria used to process calls. Examples include recorded announcements, routing criteria and timing thresholds. The calls can also be processed and channelized using the IVR System (discussed in the next subsection) in conjunction with the ACD system.

ACD also provides real-time statistics like incoming call volume, number of calls in a queue and peak calling hours, which supervisors, managers and CSRs use to fine-tune their operations.

All the above features bring a number of advantages like no busy tones, increase in CSR productivity, no tension of missing critical calls and more.

10.2.1 Features, States and Codes—All Advanced

Application Based Routing and Reporting routes calls based on the type of call or application as against the traditional way of routing and tracking by agent groups and trunk groups. An agent group is a group of agents that share common skills. An agent group is also called Skills Group or Gate. A trunk group is a collection of trunks associated with a single peripheral and usually used for a common purpose.

ACD can also route calls in an intelligent way, through the conditional "if…then" method. ACD uses various parameters and context-based inputs like the type of call, country of origin, number of agents available, etc., to perform call routing. This is referred to as Conditional Routing and it helps to improve response time.

CSR phones are equipped with the standard hold and transfer features in addition to a queue button that flashes when callers are waiting in queue and a sign offline button that allows CSRs to sign on and off the system.

When a CSR signs in, his initial ACD state is set to the default value, which is typically 'Available'. This initial state can be changed to other states either through menu options or soft keys. While in the 'Unavailable' state, CSRs can chose an appropriate reason code like 'Out to lunch' that gets appended to their state description. The wrap-up state allows CSRs to complete paperwork and other post-call processing before responding to another call; they record information like the origin of the call, final status and caller satisfaction level. CSRs use wrap-up codes to identify the nature and type of calls they are handling so that this information can be used for statistical purposes. The ACD can then generate pre-built reports for these codes.

10.3 Interactive Voice Response—Interative All the Way

Interactive Voice Response (IVR) is an automated system that provides self-service features via the phone to inbound customers. It uses features like menu options, a series of predetermined questions, prerecorded voice prompts and filtering logic to find a solution to customer problems through automated solutions or by transferring the IVR calls to the appropriate CSR or department. IVR helps to cut down call times and the cost of sales, inquiry and service.

This system communicates with the customers by following a recorded script and it captures responses of the callers based on touch-tone or voice responses given by the customers. Modern-day IVR systems also enable inputs and responses to be gathered through voice recognition.

A typical implementation of IVR is its integration with PBX services or voice mail services. Additionally, IVR proves to be very useful for disabled professionals who may have trouble pressing buttons.

Organizations are increasingly adopting IVR and to implement IVR, organizations need the following components:

A. Hardware and Software Platforms

B. A team of IVR experts who handle all the aspects of IVR like configuration, security, development, scalability, maintenance, deployment and integration

C. Telephony Infrastructure

D. Databases

10.4 Predictive Dialer System—Smart Performers

A predictive dialer is an automatic call processing system used in outbound scenarios like telemarketing, mass notifications, collection centers and market surveys. It automatically calls a list of telephone numbers based on statistical algorithms that connect CSRs to the customers. Only calls that are answered by a live person are handled; calls that reach an answering machine or play a "no longer in service" message or have a busy signal or even disconnected lines are immediately discarded.

There are three types of dialers. Hard Dialers are hardware-based systems. Though they require more equipment and maintenance, they are able to handle a large number of calls per hour. The second option is called Soft Dialers. They are software packages that rely on the processing power of computers to connect to the customers. Features like call progress analysis and call classification are all incorporated in the software itself; there is no need of any extra equipment. The last type is Intelligent Predictive Dialers. These dialers have features just like the regular dialers plus they provide intelligent integration of automatic dialing with automatic voice messaging—here whenever the dialer detects a live person, it first plays a voice message explaining the purpose of the call and prompts the live person whether he/she wants to talk to a live CSR.

10.4.1 Features and Benefits—Optimal in All Aspects

A. The main feature is to avoid having CSRs sitting idle by predicting when callers will become available to receive calls. This feature helps CSRs to move on to the next number on the list thereby ensuring that they do not waste precious time on unanswered or unsuccessful calls. It uses smart algorithms to determine the course and pattern of future calls.

B. Instead of wasting more than half of their time on unproductive calls, CSRs are able to spend the majority of their time in meeting their quotas.

C. Through real-time monitoring of various statistics like average call abandonment rate, missed calls, number of phone lines available, etc., predictive dialing performs proper queue management, focuses on potential customers and keeps a tab on the performance of each and every CSR.

D. This system generates reports on various real-time statistics like the conversational ability of CSRs, the number of calls completed by each CSR every day, call reminders, etc. These reports help the management to introduce provisions to correct performance gaps in CSR productivity.

E. Lead generation is another important benefit. This system aids in generating and controlling leads based on various factors like call backs, sales, etc. When a particular number is called by the predictive dialer system and the CSR logged a lead or a sale from that call, the system records this data for future use.

10.5 Databases—Up-to-Date Access

Databases provide easy accessibility and functionality to both customers and CSRs based on quality-checked and up-to-date information.

Database software acts as an integrator for storing, sorting and accessing all sorts of information. This information helps in reducing call volume by diverting it to alternative channels. It facilitates automatic routing of multiple channel customer queries using parameters like CSR skills, customer profile, etc. Self-help options facilitate the customers to access the database for repetitive queries.

10.5.1 Features and Benefits—Insights and Intelligence

There are various prominent features and benefits of databases:

A. They allow generation of survey questionnaires and response scoring based on the customer profile and transaction data. These surveys help call centers to learn about the customer buying habits, satisfaction levels, inputs and feedback, etc.

B. They are a knowledge base in themselves. They store information related to customer behavioral patterns and there are flagging options that help to identify responsive and non-responsive customers. Organizations leverage this knowledge hub to perform sales lead follow-up, tap new markets and reactivate dormant customers.

C. They help to store information regarding customer service requests and responses, agent skills, agent availability, shifts and support knowledge. All these aspects help in bringing about shorter call handling times and higher first-call resolutions.

D. Integration interfaces with the CRM system help to provide a single view of the customer throughout the organization.

E. They provide import and export of data, and data conversion features.

10.6 Reporting Capabilities—Measure with Accuracy

Reporting capabilities must be able to meet the reporting needs of any sized call center. These capabilities range from basic performance factors to advanced real-time reports. This system must be able to manage call history, perform call recording and management, and provide search facility. These features help to quantify call center performance. Accurate reports about various parameters like Average Handle Time, Sales Conversion, Occupancy, Average Speed of Answer (ASA is the average time it takes for a call to be answered; the average time that elapses between the time the call reaches the ACD and the time it is connected to a CSR), Total Talk Time, Hold Time, Calls Per Unit Time, % Calls Handled, and many more metrics are needed for tracking and measuring purposes.

Without reports, performance issues go undetected. Through real-time monitoring, management is able to identify both operational issues and star performers. With the help of historical reporting, managers study trends and plan new strategies. These reports capture data from sources like ACD, WFM system, Databases and CRM System in order to calculate metrics.

Advanced reporting software also has the feature of customizable reports that are generated at a specific time or interval, archived for later retrieval and e-mailed to the intended recipients.

10.7 Computer Telephony Integration—Integration of Interactions

Computer Telephony Integration (CTI) is the seamless and intelligent integration of the computer system with the telephone network. It is a sophisticated means of providing a single platform catering to all communication-related needs.

In today's times, it refers to the integration of interactions occurring over several customer contact channels like web, voice calls, chat, e-mail, etc.

The CTI software installed on the computer is in constant communication with the telephone system server to handle various aspects of call management like calling line identification, call recording and logging, putting calls on hold and transferring calls. The middleware allows you to choose how your computer application responds to each call.

10.7.1 Main Functions—All in One

Some of the main functions of a CTI system are as follows:

A. Screen pop is a useful feature that displays all the relevant customer and account information on a CSR's screen. It provides CSRs instant access to all relevant data by interfacing with a centralized database.

B. Provides interactive voice response (IVR) to the customers.

C. Synchronizes the transmission of data between telephones and computers.

D. Provides voice recognition features for either forwarding the call to an appropriate CSR or for authenticating the caller.

E. Records calls for quality purposes.

F. Provides more timely access to information.

10.8 Scripts—Script your Call Center Success

Develop scripts around the customer needs. Ensure that the scripts have the right tone and do not sound like they are being read out by CSRs. The customers like talking to a live person on a one-to-one basis, not to a recording machine. Scripts are much more than prewritten responses to common queries; they are a tool to facilitate a smooth call flow and generate a new sale.

The next factor to be kept in mind while designing scripts is that they need to be properly formatted and need to follow the *less is more* principle. Only then CSRs are able to answer promptly and confidently, without any undue delays and repeats.

Scripts should not be one lengthy monologue. They need to be worded in such a way that they evoke customer response and interest too. Bulleted points help CSRs to cover all the important points, and at the same time, also allow space and time for customer interaction. Humanizing the scripts with features like simple greetings and closing lines help to build and maintain customer rapport.

Audio reviews, customer satisfaction ratings, statistics and call logs of the interactions help to fine-tune the scripts and ensure better script delivery. Another important benefit of these reviews and ratings is that you can pinpoint whether or not the scripts sound like a long recording session. If they do, then one or more of the above features of prefect scripts are missing.

An effective script is one which maintains the customer's interest throughout the communication cycle. All the above features help you to maintain this interest.

10.9 Vendor Choices—Choose Wisely

Organizations use a variety of best-in-breed products from a variety of vendors. Many vendors handle both incoming and outgoing calls. These days due to significant market consolidation, vendors also offer call center suites. Some of the major vendors are Avaya, Cisco, Nortel and Alcatel-Lucent. Vendor choices have to be done very carefully as factors like organizational image and business agility depend on these choices too. Alignment with the business nature, operational areas, needs and size of a call center is a must.

Before signing on the dotted line, organizations need to thoroughly draw out their needs and goals, and then start matching vendors to them. By interviewing senior managers, organizations get an accurate picture of organizational needs and goals. A final buy-in from all stakeholders is needed on the final selection criteria for vendors.

At the outset, the most important fact to consider is what type of calls will be handled. The monthly minimum and maximum figures along with seasonal spikes need to be accurately defined in order to find the best suited vendor. The medium of service matters too. Depending on what kind of channels an organization is going to use to service callers—phone, e-mail, web or any other channel, the choice of vendors is made. In other words, the vendor solutions should allow you to offer the customers their choice of communication channels. The needs of your internal and external customers are a big input in developing an accurate set of requirements.

Organizations need to share with their potential vendors the information they need for them to be able to submit detailed responses. Only when organizations provide accurate and detailed information to the vendors, the vendors too will respond with the same quality of information. Open dialog is beneficial while sending out Request for Information (RFI) to potential vendors; organizations need to share their expectations about project scope, reporting, performance requirements, pricing, operational parameters, etc., with the vendors in a transparent manner. Open dialog also helps while comparing and scoring vendor responses based on organizational requirements to qualify those vendors who will receive the final Request for Proposal (RFP).

Organizations should get quotes from several sources to estimate the pricing in terms of costs and savings. This in-depth research is needed to strike a mutually beneficial relationship with vendors. Setup fee is an important factor that drives up the cost. Organizations also need to make sure that vendors spell out what additional costs are involved, for example, training, reporting fees, etc. All these aspects need to be studied before finalizing the contract terms and conditions, and pricing details. The contract is more than just pricing; it should also cater to service level agreements, penalties, confidentiality terms, monitoring rights and renewal policy.

Visiting the vendor's website gives you useful insights about the vendor's call center solutions. Visiting the physical location can give you a firsthand feel of the working climate, the kind of projects handled and the scale of operations. If physical visits are not possible, you can make your own sample calls to see how the vendor's CSRs respond. In the case of existing vendors, organizations can make calls to gauge whether the CSRs have received adequate knowledge and training about the products and services.

Security in terms of back-up facilities, disaster recovery, and measures for data security and continuity of operations is a critical issue that needs to be carefully discussed with vendors and a collective buy-in should occur.

Potential vendors should have the appropriate territory footprint, geographic reach and processes in place to meet the specific needs of geographies outside the "home" geography, either directly or through other appropriate channels and subsidiaries.

Potential vendors should be able to support the required level of customization and business transformation. The vendor's level of expertise should match the relevant areas of functioning. The vendor's architecture should be scalable enough to achieve the business goals.

Everything needs to be in black and white; all clauses, issues and instructions need to be acknowledged in writing.

All these factors provide a thorough understanding of the vendor landscape in order to make judicious choices and avoid protracted implementation schedules.

10.9.1 Evaluation—Find the Premier Partner

The following worksheet contains the various areas of evaluation that call centers need to carefully study, analyze and score before short-listing vendors. They can use the Weighted Scores method or the Percentage of Points Available Method to do so. Each call center has different weights or percentages for the sub-areas within each evaluation criterion. Based upon how well the vendor fares in each sub-area, call centers assign a score or points and then multiply the score or points by the designated weight or percentage to get the total weighted points or final score for each evaluation criterion. The bottom line is to compare and evaluate competing vendor capabilities in order to select the partner with the right skills, right technologies, right processes and right people, and all these should come at the right price.

Vendor Information (Name, Address, E-Mail, Contact Person, Website, Fax and Telephone):				
Value proposition: Main products and services: Main areas of expertise: Number of years in the business: Onshore, nearshore and offshore capabilities: Number of employees: Third party accreditations:				
Criteria (1)	**0-10 Score (2)**	**Weight (3)**	**Weighted Score (2 x 3)**	**Comments**
Organizational Values				
Cultural Fit				
Integrity				
Client Focus				
Brand Image				
Total Weighted Score				
Management				
Leadership Style				
Expertise, Commitment and Professionalism				
Level of Participation				
Industry Experience				
Total Weighted Score				
Performance and Service				
Performance History and Reputation				
Commitment to Customer Service				
Performance-driven Results Within Time and Budget Constraints				
Maintenance and Support Services				
Ease of Implementation				
Support Level for Growth and Future Service Needs				
Service Reliability				
Total Weighted Score				

(Contd...)

Terms and Conditions				
Training and Reporting Fees				
Service Level Agreements				
Renewal Policy				
Confidentiality Terms				
Special Terms for Seasonal Workload				
Legal Terms				
Warranties				
Monitoring Rights				
Total Weighted Score				
Procedures, Policies and Guidelines				
Project Management Methodology				
Working Procedures				
Communication Guidelines				
Change Management				
Quality Control and Assurance Practices				
Retention Strategies				
Knowledge Management				
Escalation Procedures				
Reporting Guidelines				
Total Weighted Score				
Training				
Ability to Meet the Training Needs				
Quality of the Training Imparted				
Quality of Training Aids				
Total Weighted Score				
Experience and Financial Position				
Key Operational and Functional Areas				
Breadth of Solutions Offered				
Vertical Focus				
Financial Stability				
Funding Position				
Total Weighted Score				
Market Value and Image				
Position in Industry				
Customer References				
Sample Calls				
Amount of Past Business				
Site Visits				
Total Weighted Score				

(Contd...)

Technology and Infrastructure				
Technology Portfolio				
Level of Technology Understanding				
Level of Support and Troubleshooting				
Third party Systems and Interfaces				
Awareness of and Adaptiveness to New Technology Trends				
Internal Infrastructure				
Level of Integration Support				
Frequency of Upgrades in Technology				
Regulatory Compliance Support				
Customization Services				
Total Weighted Score				
Staff				
Technical and Domain Expertise				
Motivation Level				
Experience				
Work Culture				
Turnover Rate				
Responsiveness				
Total Weighted Score				
Security				
Back-up Facilities				
Disaster Recovery Plan				
Measures for Data Security				
Measures for Continuity of Operations				
Total Weighted Score				
Markets and Clients				
Market Knowledge				
Client Base				
Territory Footprint				
Geographic Coverage				
International Support				
Channels and Subsidiaries				
Total Weighted Score				
Invite to RFP (Yes/No): Additional Notes:				

PART-III

Call Centers in India—The First Choice

In this part...

The history of call centers in India, reasons for the phenomenal growth of call centers in India and how this growth has catapulted India's economic status are covered.

Aspects like the current status of call centers in India and India's position in comparison to other competing nations are dealt with in this part too.

Major emerging trends and forecasts of the Indian call center space are covered in the last chapter of this part.

India—The Shining Star of Call Centers

11

Picture this: It is 9:00 a.m. in California, USA, i.e., 9:30 p.m. in Mumbai, India, when over hundreds of Indian professionals are answering customer calls or processing transactions for the overseas customers—these are typical call centers in India.

Whenever one talks about outsourcing, India is the first name that comes to everybody's mind. Global organizations have always preferred outsourcing call center services to India in comparison to other Asian nations. Some of the main reasons are that the Indian workforce is cost-oriented, fluent in English and technically sound. India has the largest number of state-of-the-art call centers in the world. Foreign multi-national organizations find India's call center solutions not only cost-effective but also globally competitive.

Despite their recent arrival on the Indian soil, call centers have witnessed explosive growth in all major sectors (travel, banking and financial services), especially in the last 3-5 years and will continue with this trend for a considerable time period. Rapid advances in telecommunications technology and the call center-friendly reforms make India the most attractive call center location.

Today, India is aptly called as the *world's outsourcing hub*. You will find twenty-somethings working in call centers at every nook and corner of the Indian subcontinent. The number of organizations setting up call centers in India has only been increasing over the years.

With the rapid expansion of the call centers, one possible problem that the Indian call centers are likely to face is a shortage of qualified English-speaking professionals. For India to overcome this problem, to remain the first choice and to lead the race of outsourcing, public investment in facilities like training, education, transportation, airports and utilities should step up to match the private investment levels.

In order to retain her position as a call center pioneer, India needs to continue building capabilities so as to attract significant amount of both domestic and international investment.

11.1 Intrinsic Strengths—Leading the Way

The call center field in India is at its peak today; it is performing well in all industries—Telecommunications, Banking, Insurance, Transportation, Hospitality and many more. There are numerous reasons that make India a major player in the call center field. There are numerous advantages and a bag-full of benefits that encourage global organizations to outsource call center services to India. They are as follows:

A. One of the most important reasons for India attracting so many call center opportunities is a vast pool of skilled and technically able manpower, which is also fluent in the English language. It also has a high-level of global awareness and is fairly comfortable with computers. This fluency helps in providing high-quality voice-based service to global customers.

B. The previous advantage is further accentuated by the fact that Indian labor comes cheap (due to the dollar-rupee exchange rate), at a low salary cost, which makes India as the most preferred destination for global giants to outsource their call center business to. The average cost per agent in India is approximately $400 per month, which is five times less than their American counterparts. Indian call center employees are highly sought after for global positions too.

C. India is the emerging knowledge capital of the world. This is further fuelled by the trend of high-tech, well-manicured parks. The country already has such parks in major cities and this trend is picking up speed in sub-metros too. The parks are self-contained mini townships in themselves, which attract thousands of knowledge workers. As all facilities are in place, these knowledge workers are free from work-related issues and are able to provide new value-added call center services. The workforce also demonstrates cultural compatibility with Western economies. This in turn attracts foreign investment.

D. Until the year 1994, the telecom sector was under the government control. In the year 1994, the Indian government announced a policy under which the sector was liberalized and private participation was encouraged. This new economic reform catapulted the growth of call center services as the deregulation of telecom industry attracted a lot of foreign interest and investment. The government policies and business settlement norms have always been call center-friendly by providing incentives, exempting tax on the export of ITES, and reducing tariff on internet services and telecom services.

E. India's incredible role in handling the Y2K problem proved India's talent in terms of a strong offshore labor force. This track record has attracted international organizations to Indian shores for establishing their presence in the call center space too.

F. Associations like Confederation of Indian Industry, Associated Chambers of Commerce and Industry of India and Federation of Indian Chambers of Commerce and Industry are also doing their bit to promote the growth of call centers.

G. India possesses a thorough knowledge of specialized services like inbound services, customer technical support, disaster recovery, e-mail and chat support, etc. Call centers in India are good at providing IT-enabled services too. Due to well-established educational and business models, call center operations and management are handled by qualified CSRs and managers. Research figures show that this operational expertise cuts down operational costs by more than half.

H. India is an ideal location to implement follow-the-sun approach. India's time zone difference is a big advantage when dealing with the developed countries of the west.

India has a 12-hour time difference with US and 6 to 7 hours with Europe. This time difference allows call centers to provide 24*7*365 service, no matter whether it is hot, snowy or rainy. Round-the-clock customer support equates to round-the-clock happy customers. Partnering with outsourced call centers in India gives the western organizations the advantage to establish themselves where they do not yet have physical presence.

I. The country today has an impressive telecom network. High-end telecom facilities and infrastructure support that are at par with global standards is another reason for India's popularity as a profitable base for outsourcing. Low cost structures enable India to use new technologies to support pre-sales and post-sales services.

J. The Indian call center turnover rates are much lower than the turnover rates in other countries like United States of America.

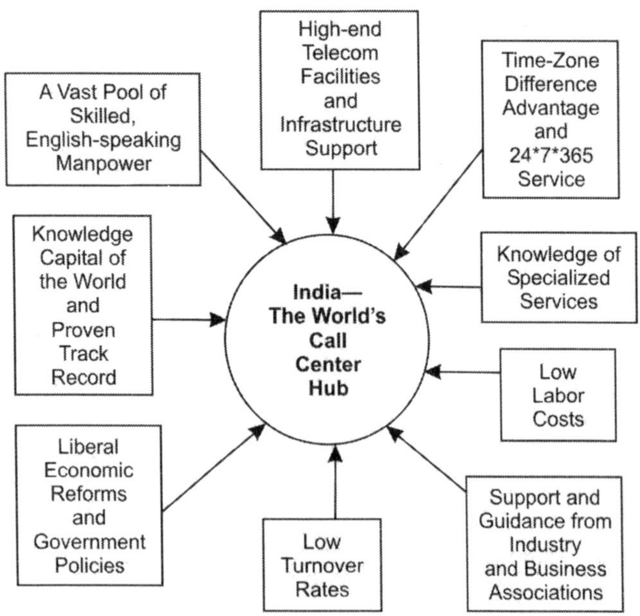

Figure 11.1: India—The World's Call Center Hub

These factors are why most fortune 500 organizations outsource to India. These factors are responsible for the creation of 'Brand India'. India has kept up the spirit of 'Glocalization' by blending the best from global business practices, strategies and models with its own work culture and performance levels (Glocalization is a combination of the words "globalization" and "localization").

11.2 Current Status—A Symbol of Economic Boom

Call centers in India represent a symbol of India's economic boom. They are also a hot topic in Indian pop culture and are a subject dealt with in the academic research field, literary circles and various motion pictures.

Call centers are flourishing in all five zones of India. In the North zone, call centers in the cities of Noida, Chandigarh, Delhi and Gurgaon are the forerunners. In South India, Chennai and Bangalore lead the race and other players like Madurai, Salem, Hyderabad, Cochin and Coimbatore are contributing their share of services too. In the Central zone, Indore and Bhopal are lucrative call center cities. In the East zone, Bhubaneswar, Patna and Kolkata reign the call center landscape, whereas in West India, Mumbai, Ahmedabad, Aurangabad, Pune, Nagpur, Nasik and Baroda rule the call center dynasty.

Table 11.1: Important Call Centers Zone-Wise

Zones	Important Call Centers
North	GE Capital, Accenture services, WNS, Convergys
South	24/7 Customer, MSourcE
Central	Aegis, Mphasis
East	Tata Sky, Accenture
West	Epicenter, Intelenet, Morgan Stanley, Sitel

Over the last decade or so, the constant rise in the Indian global presence has strengthened India's position as a value-added call center market. The call center job opportunities have helped to solve the problem of unemployment to a certain extent.

Moreover, Indian call centers are also responsible for the growth of the auxiliary services like call center training, security services and transportation. There are several call center training institutes across the length and breadth of the country that provide training in various areas like voice and accent, soft skills and process orientation.

People in India tend to have very good English skills, which gives them an advantage for outsourcing when compared to other Asian countries, where the workforce may not be as well-versed in English as their Indian counterparts. Indian call center employees have their own hybrid vocabulary. No matter whether Indian call centers are about Indianized words or the Americanized accent, the bottom line that Indian call centers follow is to focus on getting the customer problems solved.

The Indian call center workforce is omnipresent; you will find an Indian in every nook and corner of the world. If you connect to a call center anywhere in the world, including India, often you will get to hear an Indian voice at the other end of the communication link using a suitable foreign moniker or an Anglicized name, and very much keen on handling your request. "I am Usha. And the moniker I use is Ursula as it is the first name of my favorite author", says one Indian CSR. "My real name is Asha. And the pseudonym I use is Ashley", says another Indian CSR.

Illustration 11.1: The Indian Call Center Workforce is Omnipresent

In order to help call center employees to keep up with international skills and progress further in their careers, several organizations have implemented career diversification opportunities and multiple career tracks.

India is home to several premier institutes like the Indian Institute of Management and the Indian Institute of Information Technology. These institutes produce thousands of well-educated professionals in the fields of engineering, computer management and technology each year, who then go on to contribute their skills and talent in the economic space through various sectors including call centers.

The major call center cities in India are Delhi, Mumbai, Chennai, Bangalore, Kolkata, Ahmedabad and Hyderabad—these are all Tier-1 cities. Delhi being a leading city of India has seen an unprecedented rise in call centers and has call centers of big names like Wipro and American Express. Mid-sized cities are not too far behind their metropolitan counterparts and are making their presence felt in the market too. Due to the rising real estate and infrastructure costs, call centers are looking at Tier-2 and Tier-3 cities like Nagpur, Nasik, Jaipur, Mysore and many more for starting their operations. These cities are weak in infrastructure and skilled manpower; hence the government along with private organizations is working really hard to eliminate regulatory hurdles and bring about overall advancement in the operational level of call centers so as to improve the employment sector through call centers in Tier-2 and Tier-3 cities.

GE Capital, AXA Global, Morgan Stanley, Daksh eServices, Sitel, eFunds International, e-Serve, Convergys and many more boast of providing exemplary customer experiences through their fine people management models. The service arms of organizations like Dell, Accenture and many others have set up shop in India. These successful call center outsourcing ventures have encouraged more and more global organizations to outsource their call center services to India.

The range of customer services provided is mindboggling—technical support, outbound telemarketing, order fulfillment, voice mail, web chat, E-Commerce augmentation and the list goes on. There are organizations that specialize in outbound and direct response programs, and then there are organizations that deliver E-Commerce customer care too.

The Business Process Industry Association of India (BPIAI) (formerly known as the Call Center Association of India (CCAI)) was set up in the year 2001. BPIAI provides a network for members to jointly address challenges facing call centers by organizing conferences and events. It acts as a liaison with government bodies and other regulatory organizations in order to provide a boost to call centers. It taps opportunities for human resource development, technology development and career advancement.

In order to contain attrition rates and help CSRs to achieve their personal goals, organizations have implemented several innovative strategies. Organizations have tie-ups with premier educational institutions to provide distance learning education for their employees. Some organizations have gone one step further by providing scholarships to their employees to pursue their higher education goals. Organizations have also introduced several employee-oriented events to strike a work-life balance for their employees. Several call centers have also entered into non-poaching agreements to counter attrition and job hopping.

India is leaving no stone unturned to ensure that this booming sector continues to progress and provide long-term viability across verticals, products and services, and markets.

Table 11.2: The Transition of Call Centers in India

Indian call centers have come a long way:

From	To
Low-end, back-office services	Critical and complex services
Meeting external demands	Meeting global as well as domestic demands
The most preferred location	The most preferred location plus The strategic partner of global players

11.2.1 Novel Initiatives—Enabling Skills and Solutions

There are several novel call center initiatives in India that have set the trend of providing ace services by combining the best available technology, tools, processes and people.

Taking the campaign of bridging information gaps one step further is the novel venture of Kisan Call Center (KCC). KCC was launched by the Department of Agriculture & Cooperation (DAC), Ministry of Agriculture, Government of India on January 21, 2004 across the country to deliver services to the farming community. KCC is a perfect combination of modern technology and the age-old industry of agriculture. Indian farmers have turned tech-savvy and KCC has made this possible by providing subject matter expertise and instant solutions.

Piramal e-Swasthya is a healthcare initiative with an aim of providing reliable, affordable, quality healthcare facilities to the remote villages in India. Through its novel business model of combining the power of technology with the empowerment of local women, it aims at democratizing healthcare in order to give the rural population access to what many consider a luxury today. The local women are given rigorous training in various areas, right from collecting diagnostic data to customer service. These trained women also called as Sevaks (helpers) act as a quick link between villagers and the call center. The center helps to store diagnostic data and generates validated prescription and treatment details.

'EuroAble' is a state-of-the-art Mumbai-based call center established by Eureka Forbes in association with the National Society for Equal Opportunities for the Handicapped. It is a unique initiative run by people with special needs. EuroAble is India's first call center manned and operated entirely by Differently-Abled and it was launched in early 2011. This goes to show that call centers are an effective instrument in empowering people with special needs and physical challenges, enabling their talents, giving them financial independence, and integrating their skills in the mainstream value chain. The slogan of the call center is 'Spreading smiles to millions', which reflects that call centers have a humane side to them too.

E-governance departments of State machinery have announced and introduced call centers to handle several of their administrative functions. For example, making the Right to Information (RTI) accessible in remote areas through Call to

Connect India Private Limited (which is a public-private tie-up initiative) so as to ensure prompt processing of RTI applications.

To tap the immense power of search engine advertising, Google India launched a new Adwords call center in Hyderabad in 2010 with support for local languages. This platform will definitely help local business entities with their online advertising campaigns.

In early 2011, the Securities and Exchange Board of India (SEBI), the regulator for the securities market in India, decided to outsource its investor helpline service to a third-party call center. This decision was taken to resolve the rising number of investor complaints on a fast-track basis. The proposed call center would also cater to issues like IPO and trading accounts. In the long run, SEBI plans to increase the staff count from the initial 10 personnel to 1500 employees.

Bharat Sanchar Nigam Limited (BSNL), State run telecommunications giant, is all set to launch more call centers across the country to expeditiously address the complaints of its customers. It already has two main call centers—Gurgaon and Rajasthan. The Government of India's Communication Ministry is planning to introduce call centers in small cities too in order to reach out to remote customers, provide employment opportunities and improve customer service through BSNL.

11.3 Comparison—Vis-à-Vis Other Nations

When it comes to talent, India is far ahead of other competing nations such as Russia, China and the Philippines, among others.

The major competitor for India is China. China has several advantages and India needs to build its competency in these areas soon in order to sustain her position as a major call center hub. China has the potential to grow rapidly due to factors like cheap manpower, better infrastructure and growth through the Japanese outsourcing route. On the other hand, India is better in so many aspects like a large tech-savvy, English-speaking workforce, quality-driven processes and a long history of being in the call center business. The NASSCOM-Mckinsey Study 2005 says "25 percent of engineers in India have the basic skills for offshore IT jobs, compared to 10 percent each in China and Russia". China is working really hard to gain supremacy and India needs to act fast to maintain her supremacy by beginning to increase the advantages, for example, by focusing on the Japanese outsourcing route, India will be able to eat into the Chinese market share.

Malaysia, Vietnam and the Philippines are becoming serious competitors as they are low-cost locations, have a large English-speaking resource base and have a great government backing. Australia is another growing competitor due to its large English-speaking population with a favorable time zone. India too has all these advantages, but to be able to sustain the differentiation in this game, India is putting up with this competition in various ways. India is striving to provide a comprehensive range of services through vertical integration and personalized solutions. Another trend that India is encouraging is that of buying outsourcing operations in lower-cost countries.

The Philippines is a former US colony due to which it has a language advantage. Filipinos tend to speak with a more Americanized accent, whereas in India English is taught with a British dialect. But this in no way is hampering India's growth as intensive voice training is imparted across the length and breadth of the country. Moreover, India scores higher in all other areas like the number of skilled workers, government support and political stability.

According to the management consulting company, A.T. Kearney, in its 2011 Global Services Location Index (GSLI) report, India scores 7.01 overall, followed by China, Malaysia, Egypt and Indonesia in the top five destinations. Though the Philippines is a major competitor to India, it ranked number nine on the list, which is way behind India.

The Indian call centers are always talked about in political circles around the world and protested by activists in US and UK. Despite this opposition, call centers in India will continue to sustain their growth as they are a great source of economies of scale and revenue generation for foreign multi-nationals.

Year-on-year repeat contracts from global giants prove that India is still a favorite hotspot.

India is constantly on the lookout for opportunities to improve her background and understanding of this space. Indian call centers are not about mere cost-cutting, but they are about delivering strategic business value and best practices. They are focal points of initiatives for progress.

Future in India—The Call Center Specialist

12

Call centers are one of the main factors resulting in India's economic boom. Currently, it is the fastest growing sector in the Indian subcontinent and gives a great global environment to work in. Organizations that consider India for setting up call centers come with a long-term view as India's advantages in the call center arena have been tried, tested and proven. The future of call centers in India is bright and will provide a higher rate of growth in order to meet the global corporate needs.

Though Indian call center employees may have to lose a part of their identity by adopting American skins and Anglicized names, there is also a good side to this—call centers bring with them a gamut of advantages like better compensation and fast-track careers. The booming Indian call centers are definitely the next *big* thing in the world.

12.1 Major Emerging Trends—Further Growth

With a cost-efficient workforce available in India, organizations started turning towards the Indian soil, a trend started by GE when it established its call center near New Delhi in 1998. Other major players that entered the field were American Express, AT&T, British Airways, Daimler-Chrysler and so many more players, both old and new.

The call center market in India is maturing each day. It is moving towards trends like enterprise-wide centers, advanced workforce management solutions, self-service solutions and virtualization.

Call centers are growing by more than 15 percent per year, and the offshore segment is certainly among the fastest growing segments. The scope of services provided by call centers in India has increased considerably and will continue to do so.

Several collaborative ventures have experienced great financial success, for example, ONStor Inc., a major developer of storage systems based in Los-Gatos, says its tie-up with Bangalore engineering-services outfit of HCL Technologies Ltd., enables it to get customized products to the customers twice as fast as its major competitors. Collaborative ventures are another major trend. Such ventures allow small organizations to compete with global players at a lower cost and reduced lead time.

Indian call centers are gearing up for tapping the multilingual call center space. Organizations like OneSource, HCL, iGate, ICICI, etc., provide call center services in various languages in order to cater to the needs of Pan-European, Japanese, Southeast Asian, French and German customers.

Outsourcing of process management has a great potential for growth in the coming years. According to industry sources, this segment will touch the $1.6 billion mark by 2014.

With more and more call centers in India, both international and domestic, people are bound to be financially stable. The gradual penetration into rural areas means not only income generation and employment opportunities for rural people, but also setting up of native language-based call centers for Indian customers.

Today, having call centers in India has become the norm for several global giants, and industry experts believe that India will continue to have this advantage till 2018 or 2019. Some analysts predict that India's GDP is likely to grow at 8 percent to 10 percent for the next decade.

Along with providing services to the developed world, India has opened a new frontier—catering to its own growing needs. According to a recent McKinsey & Company report (McKinsey & Company is a global management consulting firm), due to this new frontier, outsourcing revenue from within India is expected to hit $95 billion by 2020, which is nearly 15 percent of the expected global market. Along with the banking, financial services and telecom sectors, other sectors like healthcare, hospitality and retail will drive the future growth of the domestic call centers.

Spotlight Tip
Call centers in India are definitely poised for expanding their capability breadth and depth in terms of strategic ventures across all industries.

12.2 Forecasts—Bright and Right

Though India faces stiff competition from countries like China, Mexico, Indonesia and the Philippines, the outlook for India looks progressive. Prominent local players are already broadening their service portfolios to keep up with the changing call center dynamics.

Recently, business megadeals worth 10 to 15 billion dollars were entered into by Indian and US organizations, and this is expected to generate 50,000+ jobs.

According to a McKinsey study, the demand for CSRs in India is projected to grow exponentially in the next few years.

According to Forrester Research, 3.3 million US jobs will have moved offshore by 2015, with more than two-thirds of those (70 percent) going to India.

Business service centers represent a large market that lies untapped. This trend is definitely picking up and is in the process of bringing about economies of scale and standardization. Business service centers help organizations that are in the process of expansion to achieve economies of scale by providing services that consolidate fragmented business operations.

Just like their western counterparts, Indian organizations too are gearing up to provide more service delivery options to cater to the customers in Europe, North America and South America.

The scope of call centers in India is vast as it provides a growth-driven platform for both non-technical and technical human resources.

The innovation factor brought about by the call center services organizations in India has fuelled the growth of this sector. Recent reports from *Times of India* (a leading Indian

English Language newspaper) also echo the same finding. Innovation is what is keeping India ahead in the game.

Several financial institutions are providing monetary resources to fuel the expansion of call centers. This funding will in turn help domestic players to broaden their services portfolio, which will help them to generate new revenue streams and to compete on the international level.

End-to-end system integration with support facility is another emerging area that is gaining momentum. End-to-end system integration with support facility projects offer IT implementation along with complete post-implementation support under the same roof.

With the growing awareness about India and her call center potential, there are a lot of young people abroad who are willing to take up jobs in India. This trend is definitely setting the pace for bilingual and multilingual call centers.

The National Association of Software and Service Companies (NASSCOM) is a premier platform for tapping the vast potential of the call center space. Its main aims are to set up call center parks and training institutions, to promote best standards, to gain government support, to facilitate the exchange of knowledge of the latest trends and developments through tie-ups with international forums, and above all to maintain India's leadership position in the call center game. NASSCOM is the premier body that acts as a consultant for the BPO/ITES sector. The proactive support provided by NASSCOM for the BPO/ITES sector has led to the inclusion of call centers in the 'Business Auxiliary Services' segment, which in turn ensures that call centers are exempted from service tax under the Finance Bill provisions. Such supportive bodies are definitely going to affect the Indian call center space *favorably*.

The Government of India too is playing its role in stabilizing call centers by wooing investors with investment-friendly tax exemptions and subsidies. The government is providing logistic and infrastructure facilities to organizations at affordable rates entering into this space. It is also providing various concessions and incentives like tax exemption on the export of ITES.

From these points, it is clearly evident that India will continue to galvanize her foothold by expanding the call center footprint in regions like North America, South America and Europe. India will continue to compete successfully in emerging international markets to sustain her unrivaled global value chain.

Management pundits advocate that India is still the destination that completely stands out as the leading market in the offshore call center outsourcing space. The discussed factors, proven global delivery models and the already successful call center outsourcing ventures will continue to attract new players to the Indian shores.

PART-IV

Fast Forward—Be Future-Ready

In this part...

You will find real life insights and experiences of professionals and industry experts, which reveal interesting and thought-provoking facts and trends about call centers.

This part also explores new horizons, what must be done by call centers to prepare for the customer of tomorrow and what are the likely global trends that call centers will witness in the future.

Real Life Insights—Through the Eyes of an Expert

13

This chapter contains real life experiences and success stories. These insights shared by call center personnel help us to realize the importance of people readiness, process clarity and organizational effectiveness in call center operations. We also get a glimpse into the future of call centers through the eyes of real professionals and industry experts.

A. Competitive Landscape: Customer Management BPO Providers

In the current economic conditions, in which clients are looking to grow their businesses while focusing on cost containment, CM BPO is embraced as a service to accelerate growth and maintain a satisfactory level of customer experience. It continues to enjoy a steady stream of buyers considering outsourcing for the first time or expanding their existing engagement in outsourced CRM or customer management processes.

Growth in capacity in the Americas, Asia/Pacific and EMEA continues to support the rise of "best shore" models, as is the case with WAH that supports changing client preferences. As we move through these turbulent times, providers must accept that the road ahead will be difficult, especially in an ever changing, dynamic and crowded marketplace.

Gartner recommends that CM BPO service providers develop and deploy go-to-market strategies that include the following six elements to improve market share in the current competitive environment:

A. Marketing executives must be more visible in the marketplace; be known for something—as a thought leader, operationally excellent, incredibly responsive, high service quality, and so on.

B. Sales and marketing executives must differentiate services by function or industry; demonstrating functional or vertical expertise resonates well, because buyers consider industry expertise a leading evaluation criterion. Buyers are looking for specialists, not generalists.

C. Be flexible and easy to do business with. Regardless of size, don't make it difficult for buyers to engage with you. Complicated or complex contracting models or processes send the wrong message about your ability to serve clients and their customers. Reduce complexity when dealing with clients.

D. Sales executives and relationship managers must offer related services in addition to sales, marketing or customer care. Consider how to improve asset utilization—utilize available capacity off-hours, especially with respect to offshore locations. For example, the day shift in India can manage e-mail or perform back-office tasks overnight for North American clients. Beware, however, of losing focus, and spreading service coverage too thinly, or opportunistically.

E. Program and process executives must continue to add complementary services. Consistently, providers offer a range of sales, marketing and custom care services; however, few can demonstrate effective, comprehensive capabilities. As clients grow into their use of CM BPO, combined offerings can blend sales, marketing, service and support functions (with services such as customer analytics). This integrated, full-life cycle capability presents a compelling opportunity to address clients' immediate, discrete need and support their emerging needs.

F. Executives must clearly determine the approach to global delivery. Developing a network of resources to serve onshore (including WAH), nearshore or offshore has become critical to maintain any semblance of price parity. However, be prepared to consolidate delivery operations when necessary, especially post-M&A to further optimize the cost of service delivery.

(*Source: Gartner—Competitive Landscape: Customer Management BPO Providers*, TJ Singh, 2010)

Tervinderjit Singh, MBA,
Lead Analyst for Asia/Pacific (AP)-based BPO research
and IT services research for ASEAN
and Research Director, Gartner, Singapore

B. They are Willing to Experiment

Most industry pundits believe that the fast pace of change in customer expectations, technologies and accepted cultural norms around access and service has only begun. As Peter Cochran, British Telecom's former head of research once put it (just as the Internet was emerging as a customer service channel), "My paradigm for the new century is a three-click, one-second, no-handbook future. Everything I desire within three clicks of a mouse, on my screen in a second, and I really don't want to read a handbook on how to do it" (speech to *Telecommute 95*).

Consider these ingredients:

- Internet/Web
- Social Media
- Mobile
- Community
- Telephone
- Fiber Optics
- Wireless
- Interactive
- Television
- Computer
- Digital
- Software
- Multimedia
- Entertainment
- Global
- Pagers
- Virtual reality
- Networks
- Personal assistants
- Time
- Quality of life

In coming months and years, these components will be combined in numerous, yet-to-be-imagined ways. The most successful call centers continually review and reassess how they do things and the results they are achieving. What can be improved? What should be scrapped? What assumptions no longer make sense? What can be done differently? Can an outsider do it better or more efficiently? They learn from their mistakes and are constantly testing new approaches.

Even in these early stages of moving from a relatively fragmented environment of separate contact alternatives to one that is integrated, multimedia-based and intuitive, important lessons are emerging:

Lesson One: You Need a Leader. Call centers are learning that an overly democratic process can be an impediment to bold and timely decisions. Yes, cross-functional teams are vital to buy-in and implementation. But you ultimately need someone who has the authority to say, "Enough study on the matter. This is the direction we're going."

Lesson Two: Keep Your Eye on Traffic Redistribution. Accurate forecasting is the basis for staffing and skill needs, technology requirements and budgets. But it's pretty tough to know exactly how new access alternatives will impact the call load requiring live agents. This makes careful tracking even more critical and necessary. The trends in total contacts and changes in the proportion of each type of contact is a critical early-warning system.

Lesson Three: If in Doubt, Consider Getting Started with New Access Capabilities. Yes, tomorrow's technologies and our understanding of them will be much improved. But recognize that the risk associated with moving forward may be less than the risk of sitting on the sideline waiting until everything shakes out. Just getting started—e.g., with social media, deeper data analysis, improved organizational structure, multimedia capabilities, or other areas that make sense for your organization—gets you moving on the learning curve.

Lesson Four: Drive out Fear. This was a theme the late W. Edward Deming spoke of passionately, especially in his later years, and is one of his famous "Fourteen Points." Of course, there are those things that we should be fearful of, such as the consequences of being dishonest, or grossly irresponsible. But it's the wrong kind of fear, such as the fear of taking reasonable risks or the fear of constructive dissent that effective call center managers work so diligently to abolish. Fear inhibits innovation.

Lesson Five: Take Action. If there's one overall lesson, it's to take action. Despite looming uncertainties in the economy—or perhaps because of them—this is not the time to sit back and see what happens. If you do, you will be left behind. By taking calculated risks in rolling out new services, you'll be learning lessons that will help guide your organization into the next era. With many initiatives, you can often start small—but get started.

(*Source: Special Report: Twelve Traits of the Best Managed Call Centers*, Brad Cleveland, 2011)

Brad Cleveland,
Senior Advisor,
International Customer Management Institute (ICMI),
Award-winning Author of *Call Center Management On Fast Forward: Succeeding in Today's Dynamic Customer Contact Environment*
and Renowned Keynote Speaker

C. Are You Measuring the Wrong Things?

The very helpful customer service rep was the epitome of professional. She was pleasant, thorough and genuinely wanted to help me resolve my problem.

However, her company's computer system wouldn't let her.

The reason for my call was to set up automatic payments for my new mortgage. I had used their automatic phone tree to set up the payment, but the system told me I'd pay a $5 late fee even though I was doing this two weeks in advance.

I then tried doing it online, as I have for nearly all of my other accounts. I laboriously filled out all the required information. But the system kept refusing to accept my information, telling me to contact customer support.

The helpful rep walked through the process and it wouldn't let her do it either. Only by her asking her supervisor did we learn that the system won't let the customer set up an automatic payment until after the first payment.

Go figure.

Why didn't the web site state that? Why didn't the phone system tell me that? Why did I have to waste 30 minutes trying to do something the company wants—to get paid on time every time?

So the company in question has hired and trained very good customer service reps. But then it shoots itself in the foot by having systems that don't allow the customers, let alone the reps, do what they want to do, and then make the information as to why not hard to get.

But here is the clincher.

I was emailed a survey afterward. After-service surveys are good. But the design was bad. It asked only how the customer service rep behaved. She was stellar as far as she could go in getting through the irrational system. When it asked if she resolved the problem, I had to say no, as the system wouldn't allow her to solve the problem.

There were no survey questions on how the system served or failed me. If there had been, the company would have gathered valuable information on how their lack of customer-focused systems had irritated this new customer. They will keep annoying customers because they have no idea their system is broken—unless their very good customer service reps take the initiative to report it. And if someone takes their report seriously.

- Are you measuring the wrong things?
- Do you have a way to get customers' feedback on all customers' touch points, not just a live person's interaction?
- If not, you may have some glaring holes that will continue to drive your customers away, no matter how much you spend on customer service training.

Rebecca Morgan, CSP, CMC,
Best-selling Author of *Calming Upset Customers: Stay in Control in Any Situation,*
International Consultant, Speaker
and Workplace Effectiveness Expert

D. End-to-end from Hire to Retire

With the greatest challenge facing the outsourcing industry being talent acquisition and retention, it precipitates as an imperative for the different BPO organizations to adopt and implement fair, attractive and robust HR Practices. This combined with the fact that most outsourcing firms trace their roots to some old, evolved organization hailing from a developed country, the HR practices employed by the BPO industry rivals any other.

Organizations with the best HR Practices attend to the employee experience life cycle with confidence—end-to-end from Hire to Retire.

Hiring: First impressions do matter; hence the experience of a candidate during the hiring and consequent induction needs to be attended to in details. Even rejected candidates who see high standards, fairness, speed and proper feedback can become brand ambassadors for the company.

Orientation: Most companies have mandated New Hire Orientation for newbies to ensure proper understanding of the organization history, values, structure and policies.

Weekly/Monthly One-on-One Sessions: A one-on-one session with immediate manager is a must as it keeps track of the employee performance with effective feedback given to improve the same.

Open Door Policy: Adequate transparency is ensured by developing a flat organization in which employees can reach out to higher leadership to highlight any concerns, personal or otherwise.

HR/Leadership Skips: A high ranking HR official needs to conduct skips with employees once in a quarter or so to feel the pulse of the operations environment and receive feedback for developing improvement plans. This also acts as a controllership measure towards the functioning of operations and compliance to employee well-being.

Annual Appraisals: Annually, employee performance should be fairly rated with each and every employee being given adequate opportunity to highlight his/her achievements and development areas. This, in most cases, also helps to decide the employee performance bonus.

Optimum Incentivization: Prudent incentive structures should be designed and adhered to in which flawless teamwork, great performance and professional conduct are rewarded thereby encouraging others to excel as well.

Rewards and Recognition: Any extra contribution towards the business or an impactful initiative needs to be rewarded and recognized through appreciation or gifts.

Code of Conduct: Organizations that have a robust code of conduct laid down and deal with deviations fairly and swiftly always do well. A no-backlash policy ensures that employees do not fail to highlight cases of discrepancies. This includes lack of professional behavior, harassment and misconduct with colleagues, company data compromise, privacy violations, etc.

Employee Development: Managers are also rated on how they empower and develop the talent in their teams. Managers should ensure that there is enough focus on employee development and career pathing.

Personality development/Education at Work: Organizations need to invest heavily in employee personality development through in-house trainings and sessions like communication skills, time management, etc. Employees wanting to further their education level must be helped by their organization in getting professional certifications/MBA degrees from institutes of repute through tie-ups. Such education cost also needs to be subsidized or reimbursed.

Rajiv Ranjan (Human Resources),
Vcare Corporation, India

E. Future Trends in Cross-Cultural Call Center Communications

From the 1990s, an exponential number of telephone-based customer service centers in countries such as the United States (U.S.) and the United Kingdom (U.K.) have been outsourced to India and the Philippines—two English as a Second Language (ESL)-speaking countries located in Asia with a wealth of human resources and relatively low labor expenses. As a consequence, most callers in the U.S. and the U.K., who are predominantly native speakers of English, have experienced cross-cultural interactions in customer service (e.g., troubleshooting malfunctioning equipment or ordering a replacement part) with offshore agents often with varying levels of outcomes. I have worked with a U.S.-owned, third party call center company with operations in India and the Philippines since the early 2000s and have done extensive research on the language of outsourced call centers. I believe that there is a pressing need to develop more language and performance-based research to help Indian and Filipino call center agents address the primary needs of their customers. Chitra Lele's book, *Call Center Essentials: A Practical Guide to Real-Time Results*, certainly contributes to the growing number of academic and professional training literature and studies intended for offshore agents and trainers.

Unlike in other cross-cultural business settings such as teleconferencing in multi-national company meetings or negotiations in international commerce and trade, transactional communications in outsourced call centers have clearly-defined roles, power structures, and standards against which the satisfaction levels of customers during and after the transactions are often evaluated (Cowie & Murty, 2010; Lockwood, Forey & Elias, 2009). Offshore agents' "performance" in language and explicit manifestations of pragmatic skills, therefore, are scrutinized closely when defining "quality" during these outsourced call center interactions. Cross-cultural communication in customer service has become an everyday phenomenon in the U.S. and the U.K. as callers come into direct contact with agents who do not share some of their basic assumptions and perspectives. Thus, for Indian and Filipino agents, this form of communication requires: (1) language proficiency in English, (2) cultural awareness related to customer contexts, (3) knowledge and skills in transferring and understanding technical and specialized information, and (4) pragmatic skills in localizing support and accommodating requests or complaints and potential performance limitations of speakers (e.g., in troubleshooting equipment) (Friginal, 2009). All these communicative skills clearly call for more focused training and continuing experience "on the floor" with customers.

According to Pandey (2011), "India and outsourcing have become synonymous in the minds of many" (p. 14), a global perception which is in part triggered by popular film, television, print media, and news and academic coverage in the last decade. The Philippines has also become one of the major global centers for U.S.-based outsourcing owing to its call center voice-based services (Angara, 2011; BPAP, 2010). Over the last 15 years, both India and the Philippines have successfully established their reputation for delivering reliable call center services to foreign companies (Tschang, 2005). It is evident that many investors recognize these countries' advantages and capabilities in maintaining call center operations for English-speaking customers. The first two decades of outsourced call centers in India and the Philippines brought investment money and provided jobs for many skilled professionals in these two countries. It may be difficult to confidently predict the sustainability of outsourced call centers outside of the U.S. or U.K. over the next coming 10 or so years, given the many economic challenges faced by the industry. However, monetary realities and basic business intangibles still indicate that outsourcing is a very viable option. The cost of manpower and technology required to provide telephone-based customer services is far too great vis-à-vis the available offshore alternatives. It is possible, in my opinion, that customers will adjust and accommodate what they perceive to be the limitations of foreign agents in language and cultural awareness during service transactions. India and the Philippines could maintain their "healthy competition" in staffing U.S./U.K. call centers as they continue efforts to produce outcomes that are satisfactory to these corporations and customers. From my experience, high-level English competence in this context is necessary, but this alone does not determine success in transaction handling and accuracy. Cross-cultural training for agents will have to continue to develop continually as agents try to provide efficient service. Other factors that will ensure effective delivery of service such as establishing rapport, personalization of support, comprehension, and correctness of information in transactions given to callers are all equally important (Friginal, 2007).

References

Angara, E. (2011, July 4). Lacking direction. *Manila Bulletin*, A12.

[BPAP] Business Processing Association Philippines (2010). [Homepage on the Internet] Philippines: The new outsourcing hub. Retrieved March 21, 2010 from http://www.bpap.org

Cowie, C., & Murty, L. (2010). "Researching and understanding accent shifts in Indian call center agents". In G. Forey & J. Lockwood (Eds.), *Globalization, Communication and the Workplace* (pp. 125-146). London: Continuum.

Friginal, E. (2007). "Outsourced call centers and English in the Philippines". *World Englishes, 26* (3), 331-345.

Friginal, E. (2009). *The Language of Outsourced Call Centers: A corpus-based study of cross-cultural interaction.* Philadelphia: John Benjamins Publishing Company.

Lockwood, J., Forey, G., & Elias, N. (2009). "Call center communication: Measurement processes in non-English speaking contexts". In D. Belcher (Ed.), *English for Specific Purposes in Theory and Practice* (pp. 143-164). Michigan: University of Michigan Press.

Pandey, A. (2011). "Hyperpoliteness versus hypopoliteness in the era of outsourcing: Crossing the continuum from the phonetic to pragmatic". *International Journal of Communication, 21(1),* 13-52.

Tschang, T. (2005). The Philippines' IT-enabled services industry. Retrieved April 22, 2006 from http://siteresources.worldbank.org/INTPHILIPPINES/Resources/Tschang-word.pdf

Eric Friginal, Ph.D.,
Assistant Professor,
Department of Applied Linguistics and ESL,
Georgia State University (USA) and
Best-selling Author of *The Language of Outsourced Call Centers: A corpus-based study of cross-cultural interaction*

Where Do You Go From Here—New Horizons

14

Outsourcing will continue to grow. Call center trends keep changing with the times. Call centers will change in the next five years as they have in the past five. On a global scale, International Data Corporation expects that the outsourced customer care services market will reach the 66+ billion mark in 2015.

No matter where your call center is, you need to be prepared to adapt it to the current hyper-competition and future changes. With thousands of customers and organizations becoming a part of this growing fraternity, new and smart marketing approaches are reconfiguring the call center terrain. We need to remember that there is no one-size-fits-all solution. Each and every player in the call center space will need to design their own innovative, made-to-order strategies to cope with pressures of the future. The call center space is expected to witness rapid growth in the near future. Trends, head-turning changes and speculations about the global future of call centers are discussed in this chapter.

14.1 Offshore Revolution and New Technologies—Cutting-Edge Services

Call centers that have tasted success with the traditional technologies will need to make room for the influx of new ideas and techniques to meet their aggressive customer acquisition goals. The traditional call center with rows of agents in headsets answering calls is becoming obsolete. Call centers are on the cutting-edge of an ever-changing technological revolution. They are moving from rigid hardware-driven systems to scalable, sophisticated software-driven setups. Call centers are no more about just vertical markets; they are much more than that. Demand for higher-end services that require more technical knowledge is expected to grow faster than purely voice-based customer services in the years ahead.

The customers have higher expectations than they did ten years ago. New technologies will continue to give rise to virtual call centers. The growth of Internet-driven businesses will definitely have an impact on the way call centers operate. Call centers can keep up with the dynamic changes only when they are willing to reinvent themselves, *continuously*.

As the rate of customer service and retention happening through social media increases, call centers too will need to gear up for social media-oriented interfaces. These interfaces provide hassle-free and easy services without losing the communication context. Major organizations like Siemens are helping call centers to integrate social media channels into their customer service strategies by providing them with integration service solutions.

Real-time, internet-based feedback techniques and the demand for voice services will continue to rise in order to handle new modes of interaction. Every minute detail of customer interaction like authentication will be handled through voice print analysis. Current voice-related systems either provide basic functionality or need a lot of customization.

Online sales lead generation through Web 2.0 is becoming very popular in the call center world and will continue to grow in popularity as it is interactive in nature and its integration capabilities enable to plug in software modules effortlessly and to identify prospective customers effectively. This seamless integration provides both customers and employees the flexibility to operate in a seamless world. Web 2.0 provides a holistic approach for collecting customer feedback across channels. This definitely will lead to an increase in investment in technology—a trend that is already in progress.

Automated solutions alongside offshore agents will be a major trend. We will see greater integration of products in the immediate future, for example, sophisticated menus with speaker-independent speech recognition along with traditional touchtone IVR.

The demand for Bluetooth-enabled headsets that help to interconnect computers, mobiles, iPhones and many other devices is on the rise. More and more organizations are becoming aware of the fact that headsets are not just fancy accessories, but an important part of call center operations. These headsets let you work hands-free and let you seamlessly switch between mediums. Noise canceling headsets are becoming popular too; they are headsets equipped with technology that reduces background noise. Organizations are expected to make significant investment in headsets in the coming years.

Investment patterns are changing; organizations are shifting their spending from traditional technologies to hosted solutions and self-service solutions. According to the 2010 Call Center Outlook Survey Results, organizations gave the highest priority to technology investment followed by process improvement and then training and other factors for achieving their organizational mandate. On-demand call centers are fast becoming popular. In fact, they are more efficient than premises-based call centers as they provide a rich set of services at lower costs and higher efficiency, for example, hosted solutions provided over the Internet in the form of Software-as-a-Service (SaaS). According to the Gartner research group, at least 75 percent of customer service centers will use some form of SaaS application by 2013.

Earlier only organizations with a huge investment muscle could set up call centers, but now even smaller organizations are getting into this space.

There is booming growth in each and every aspect of call center functioning—CRM software, toll-free traffic, infrastructure and equipments, specialized services, etc. The next-generation customer experience is all about call center re-engineering.

14.2 Preparing for the Customer of Tomorrow—The SFS Factors

Just as call center operations and processes are undergoing a transformation, so is the customer mindset. For example, a few years ago the customers were not ready to put up with accent faux pas, but now they have become much more accommodative.

With increased customer expectations, complex transactions and cut-throat competition, the three main factors that will determine the future course of call centers are *Scalability, Flexibility* and *Sustainability (SFS)*. SFS is about simplifying the nature of customer interactions.

The customers are becoming more and more demanding, and well-informed of the market and its offerings. They want to be serviced through multi-channel environments. Organizations will need to constantly upgrade their workflows and processes, and do something off the block in order to meet the expectations of the next-generation customers. They will also need to apply new ideas and methods of working from a technology perspective. This is necessary in order to ensure that the customers continue to hold a high opinion of the value proposition of organizations and are given consistent treatment across channels.

Skills-based routing is another major aspect to raise the SFS factors. As more and more organizations join the call center bandwagon, they will need to take care of global customer needs, customer demographics and latest trends. For doing so, they will have to incorporate skills-based routing based on more granular characteristics in their corporate culture to align their agent skills with the customer needs on a global level. Another parameter used for matching agents with customers is personality. The days of simply assigning callers to agents on a first-in-first-out basis are almost over. Now, it is more about matching agents and customers based upon various attributes by leveraging computing power through various superior technologies like neural networks.

Unwanted cold calling is a dying trend. Therefore, call centers will need to find innovative ideas and processes to capture the customers. The trend is that of pulling the customers towards your call centers and not of pushing your products and services in the market. Tapping the customers online is the key to capitalizing on this trend.

Preparing for the customer of tomorrow is about "completeness of vision" and "people, processes, tools and techniques to achieve it". It is about tracking customer communication across a range of mediums and then using this information to produce solutions that will keep up with the latest trends.

14.3 Global Trends—Goal-Oriented and Value-Driven

Earlier call center operations were narrowly defined and tightly focused, but now they are evolving exponentially to conquer uncharted and unfamiliar paths. They are beginning to get their due place of recognition and are participating in the decision-making process.

They are no more looked at as just a sales and marketing department. They too are actively participating in shaping up the corporate agenda and generating results on the lead management front. This transformation from a cost center to a revenue-generating profit center is slowly and steadily picking up momentum. A profit center is a department or business unit that contributes to the overall financial results of an organization. It has the capability of producing profits on its own. Obviously, this new type of call center will not happen overnight. Organizations will need to drive this transformation through a variety of factors like developing specific areas of expertise by using the right kind of goal-oriented personnel, value-driven tools and value-driven technologies.

The ability to localize and personalize customer services in all emerging scenarios, right from cloud-based models to social CRM is the key to successfully build and implement new capabilities.

The only way to build revenue streams is by nurturing your best customers and by keeping up with current business scenarios and global trends. While preparing for global trends, call centers need to work out answers to the following questions:

A. Where are the next major market opportunities for call centers?

B. What will be the new strategies for achieving customer retention goals?

C. How will traditional methods of customer service like phone, chats, etc., and modern internet-based social networking be integrated?

D. Which call center types and sizes will attract the highest investments?

E. Will the human touch provided by CSRs be completely eliminated?

F. What new tools will be needed to project the future customer base?

G. What role will public policies and private initiatives play in shaping the future of call centers?

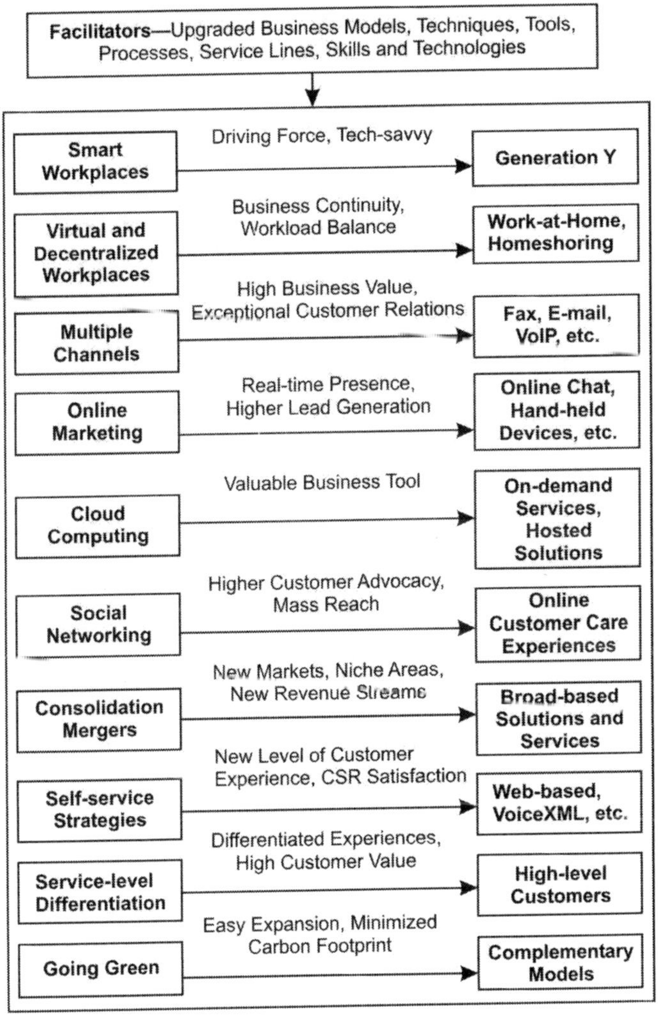

Figure 14.1: The Call Center Trends

As more and more countries get involved, speech recognition and speech automation systems are bound to get upgraded, *continually*.

Introducing multiple channels of customer contact through a single unified platform is really the next logical move in taking the customer experience to a whole new level altogether. Organizations are working hard to build such integrated platforms that will cater to all call center needs, right from routing to recording and from live monitoring to sharing real-time information. A multi-channel call center is a facility that the customers can reach through multiple channels like Web Chat, SMS, E-mail, Fax, and many more options including the traditional telephone route. This next level of service results in a string of benefits like exceptional customer relations, consolidated view of customer interactions, and consistent and speedy responses.

Advanced call forecasting modules will be used widely to capture call forecasts at shorter intervals whereby customer wait time is utilized in an optimized manner. Forecast updates could be as current as 10-15 minutes ago.

Customer Service + Social Networking = Great Pockets of Opportunities. Many organizations have come to realize the power of combining social networking and their services as a powerful combination for reaching out to new markets. Voice and data convergence will continue to happen at a much faster pace. The customers are not just "blogging" or "tweeting" about their lives; they are sharing their customer care experiences too. Social networking tools provide a better view of customer intelligence, and if call centers are able to leverage this intelligence, they can expect to see a rise of 15 percent to 50 percent in their profits. Organizations need to realize that if social networking is a medium through which the customers can complain about products and services, then this very same medium and its mass reach can be leveraged to achieve customer advocacy.

Multi-vendor networks will be on the rise. These networks help to leverage existing PBX investments and provide seamless integration of operations, which in turn eliminate unnecessary tradeoffs. Vendors are already in the process of increasing their bouquet of offerings.

As a greater percentage of the call center workforce comprises of Generation Y tech-savvy individuals, organizations will definitely need to prepare "technology-driven" and "smart" workplaces that appeal to the Generation Y's working style. For example, Generation Y is more inclined towards multiple mode-based communications, so organizations need to take this aspect into account while designing their recruitment process, workforce optimization strategy and training programs. Generation Y is the future of the call center workplace; it is the driving force behind call centers. Therefore, organizations will need to gear up to bridge the generational divide between the Generation X management personnel and the Generation Y employees. Moreover, Y-ers prove to be greatly advantageous in today's environment of multiple channels; they are well-versed in all the latest channels of communication.

The dependency on IT-enabled call centers will increase. This increase will need new skills and training to operate in an automated environment. CSRs that are skilled in phone-based communication scenarios will need to be trained in writing skills too in order to handle fast picking up trends like web-based chat. There will be significant increase in proactive customer contact activity through Internet integrated contact centers that support collaborative browsing—a form of web collaboration in which CSRs assist their customers in using a website. Research shows that automating operations through IT results in huge cost savings. Automated operations cost 2 cents to 20 cents as compared to operations handled by live agents which cost 2 dollars to 10 dollars.

Workforce optimization is another major area that is gearing up at a high pace to meet customer expectations in all areas of operations like recording, scheduling, mentoring, etc. Experiential learning imparted through learning providers is surely going to occupy a central place in future CSR development programs.

According to the U.S. Bureau of Labor Statistics, jobs for CSRs are expected to grow by about 18 percent for the period 2008-2018. This is a faster rate than the average for all other industries. Another statistics figure predicts that approximately

3.3 million US jobs will be outsourced to Southeast Asia and Africa by 2015.

According to research by Frost & Sullivan (Frost & Sullivan is a business research and consulting firm), the number of Asia Pacific call centers is expected to swell from 21,360 to 39,247 by the end of 2011. This growth is possible due to various reasons like the scalability of operations and the quality of services provided by the outsourcing market in the Asia Pacific region.

The customer base is increasing on one side of the call center equation, while on the other side, sales and service is increasing too. Due to this trend, call centers are continuing to grow in importance and are no longer being treated as a mere customer service division, but are considered as a profit center with a sales quota to meet.

Organizations will need new strategies like service-level differentiation to capture larger market shares. Service-level differentiation is a strategy for identifying high-value customers and then providing them with high-level services and differentiated experiences. It is about differentiating the customers based on their needs and then assigning CSRs to service the high-value customer needs in a personalized manner. CSRs will need to anticipate customer needs and contact them before they contact their call center. There will be more focus on handling on-hold time by identifying areas where excessive hold times can be reduced; finding time "pockets" in the main schedule where CSRs are available is one way of optimization. Call centers will need to get on their toes and work out ways on how to move forward the transaction during the on-hold period even before a CSR enters the scene. According to Accenture research (Accenture is a global management consulting firm), organizations that have optimized their support channels to differentiate service by customer value have seen revenues rise by 2 percent while reducing operating costs by 8 percent.

Consolidations and mergers among call centers will continue to occur. These consolidations and mergers help to expand their capacity in providing services and addressing requirements of new markets, especially in the case of small players in the call center field. They also lead to an increase in diversification in terms of broad-based solutions and services.

Given the rate at which fuel and commutation costs are increasing, organizations will encourage Homeshoring; Homeshoring is a practice where organizations utilize home-based employees within their country to handle call center work rather than outsourcing it outside their country. The same scenario will be applicable to the aging workforce. Virtual and decentralized workplaces will become more and more popular in the days to come as they offer business continuity, a flexible, engaging and productive work environment, and workload balance. The call load can be balanced and shifted among geographically dispersed locations in the event of disasters or technical problems in order to ensure business continuity.

As data gets more classified with each passing day, data security and data security standards will need to become more robust in terms of building and maintaining a secure network, implementing strong access control measures and implementing a foolproof vulnerability management policy.

Another trend which is going to keep going strong is the trend of online marketing. This in turn will lead to an increase in the development and deployment of online chat support software. Along with it, survey-based functionalities and hand-held mobile device applications will also be picking up. Nowadays, call centers are more about lead generation and less about call answering. To improve lead generation, call centers will need to cater to the customers of today's tech age; the customers who are connected to hand-held device applications like iPhone, Blackberry, etc. Lead generation and follow-up through e-mails and other online methods is becoming more and more widespread as it helps to provide connectivity and real-time presence between the customers and CSRs—anywhere, anytime!

Cloud computing, CRM tools and text mining programs are steadily gaining ground. As the customers are becoming tech-savvy, such new models of customer service are needed to capture services/products-related customer blog entries, social networking website wall comments and tweets.

Gartner predicts that in the immediate future, managing web interactions will be a core competency of call centers. The newest web technologies will help organizations to store their customer data and access it from anywhere in the world thereby adding another layer, another dimension to the customer experiences.

Organizations are concentrating more and more on multi-blended solutions and technologies to provide seamless customer-centric services. Multi-blended solutions also provide cost control to organizations. Apart from cost control, these solutions help to provide flexible and adaptable services to the customers in a multitude of ways. These solutions provide continuity of services even in case of unforeseen service interruptions. All these plus points are encouraging organizations to introduce multi-blended solutions.

Along with the expansion of English call centers, there is a growing demand for multilingual call centers, for example, Pan-European call centers. The main reason for this next wave is the number of people speaking different languages is growing and so is their demand for bilingual and multilingual call centers. Call centers with support for languages like French, Spanish and German are burgeoning at a high rate. According to a study conducted by the Yankee Group (Yankee Group is a technology research and consulting firm), there is a great growth potential for call centers in Australia and Europe in the coming years.

Self-service strategies like Web Self-service, VoiceXML (VXML) and Dual-tone Multi-frequency signaling are becoming the norm for increasing customer satisfaction and reducing operational costs; the customers get the opportunity to shape their own experiences. Self-service is about giving the customers the choice of waiting in queues or helping themselves through a self-service application. Self-service applications with multilingual support will also do well unabated. Developing and developed markets are embracing mobile self-service solutions. It is about providing a visual experience on the mobile handset in solving customer problems in the self-service mode. This new level of customer experience generates advantages like prevention of agent burnout and faster customer service. This new level also lets call centers focus their time and efforts on more complex operations. This does not mean that live agents will not be needed as self-service solutions are machines and have capability limited by what has been programmed into them. Organizations will need to invent approaches to blend live agents and self-service capabilities to get the best of both worlds.

Going green in call centers is becoming a big trend in itself. For this trend to become a hit in the true sense, organizations need to rise above the PR of environmentalism. Going green must become everybody's responsibility in call centers. Environment friendliness through green initiatives in the form of E-waste management, application optimization, energy efficient data centers, energy management, recycling, shared resources across departments, agent-less transactions, etc., is becoming more of a norm than exception. Complementary outsourcing models of Work-at-Home agent capabilities and Remote agent programs will be the next big thing in building a green work environment, in minimizing the carbon footprint of call centers, and in enabling call centers to add CSRs as the business grows without having to expand existing facilities or build new ones.

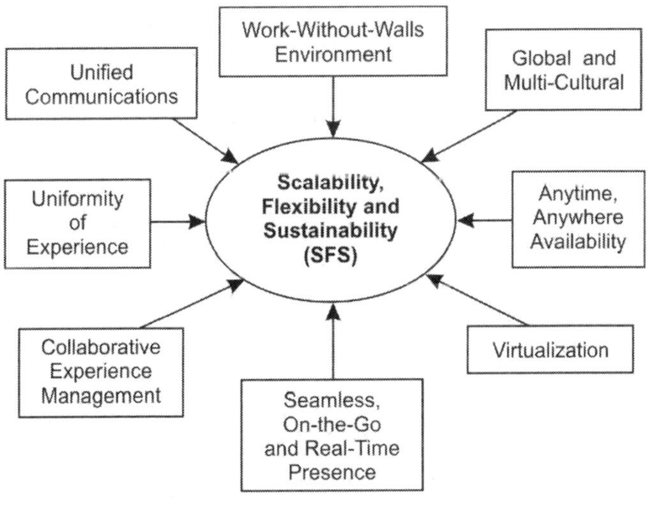

Figure 14.2: The SFS Factors

14.3.1 The Final Word—Upgrade Now!

Organizations open to new trends will find exciting opportunities and new growth models along the way. Early adopters of new technologies will witness increased competitive differentiation.

Green initiatives, social CRM tools, cloud computing, video kiosks, interactive intelligence products, television shopping, wireless media, video conferencing and self-service channels are the future. They are the means to achieving the equation of having the right CSRs, handling the right customers, at the right time, and at the right cost. Organizations that give their customers the channels and flexibility to complete tasks themselves will benefit the most.

In this fast-paced, shrinking world, developing nations hold tremendous promise for new outsourcing contracts, especially in sectors like information technology and financial services.

Whatever the current fads, marketing gimmicks and trends are, the top two key drivers that will determine the course of the call centers of the future are customer retention and customer satisfaction. Treat the customers as a partner and respect their intelligence; this is the new global business strategy. This is not just wishful thinking but a reality in many organizations.

For achieving social media maturity, organizations will need to identify the relevant social media channels and incorporate them, and constantly reconfigure themselves based on industry research and expert advice. Connecting the social and physical scenarios by inculcating best practices into each other's domain is required to survive in the social media landscape. In a recent study by the Society of New Communications Research (SNCR is a research and education foundation and think tank), 59 percent of the respondents said they regularly use social media to "vent" out their own customer service frustrations, 72 percent said they use social media to research an organization's reputation for customer service before making a purchase and 74 percent choose to do business with organizations based on the experiences shared by others online. In the similar manner, call centers can use social media to make a "social sale" by extracting valuable knowledge about a prospect prior to making a sale. Appropriate training modules need to be designed in order to cater to this aspect. Practical, comprehensive training ensures that employees are able to grasp the real meaning of what is said and done through various social media. Perfect CRM technology needs to be in place to monitor social networks, aggregation websites, community forums, blogs, wall comments, RSS (Really Simple Syndication) feeds and discussion boards.

In an era of the World Wide Web and in a world where information technology has become the new backbone of global business, restructuring of call centers seems inevitable. Call centers that bring about transformation in organizational policies, management mindset and employee attitudes will be able to sustain themselves in the world of virtualization—data, voice, video and mobility. Virtual call centers will become more prevalent in the coming years.

Organizations that will offer not only customer service to their own customer base, but also extend that customer service to their customers' customers, will be in great demand.

The above trends are about replacing a commodity-driven mindset with world-class solutions. These trends are about innovating service and sales across a growing range of channels, and giving the customers the real-time accessibility and response they demand.

A Word of Caution
Organizations need to grow with the trends in an incremental fashion so that they can win new competitive battles. The big bang approach is not that effective when it comes to realizing long-term gains.

The market for call centers is definitely poised to grow. The time to upgrade business models, techniques, tools, processes, service lines, skills and technologies is NOW!

Appendix A—Details of Call Center-Related Organizations

There are several leading business and industry associations across the world that promote and support call centers in various areas like benchmarking, operations management, service excellence, professional development, research and many more areas. These associations are considered as industry champions and thought leaders. Information on some of these bodies is shared below:

A. Business Process Industry Association of India (BPIAI) (formerly known as the Call Center Association of India (CCAI)) provides a robust network for members to jointly address challenges facing call centers by organizing conferences and events. BPIAI acts as a liaison with government bodies and other regulatory organizations in order to provide a boost to the Indian call centers.

B. Customer Care Institute (CCI), USA, is an organization that focuses on issues related to customer care and service thereby helping customer care professionals to perform better. This organization conducts surveys and research on customer care, performs customer care measurement and assessment, organizes training workshops and has many more resources to improve customer loyalty.

C. Customer Contact Association (CCA), UK, is a leading global association that provides membership services and resources to over 900 organizations. Services like CCA Global Standard© Network, Customer Experience Council, Industry Council, and Online Learning and Support help the members to gain mutual insights. It provides a platform for shared learning and aids members to overcome their performance gaps.

D. Call Center Network Group (CCNG), USA, is a dedicated body that provides a peer-to-peer platform for call centers. It enables call center professionals to enhance leadership competencies, to network with each other, to share industry trends and insights, and to exchange knowledge of tools, processes and best practices. CCNG is about connecting, sharing, and growth.

E. Customer Operations Performance Center Inc. (COPC), USA, is a globally recognized call center consulting, certification, training and benchmarking organization.

F. Incoming Calls Management Institute (ICMI), USA, is a comprehensive repository of case studies, white papers, best practices, industry news, training and certification, conferences, webinars, webcasts, forums and events. ICMI provides expert consultation and solutions in areas of workforce management, operational excellence, customer experience management and process improvement.

G. National Association of Software and Service Companies (NASSCOM), India, is a premier platform for tapping the vast potential of the call center space. Its main aims are to set up call center parks and training institutions, to promote best standards, to gain government support, to facilitate the exchange of knowledge of the latest trends and developments through tie-ups with international forums, and above all to maintain India's leadership position in the call center game.

H. Society of Workforce Planning Professionals (SWPP), USA, is a leading organization that provides a network of great support to the workforce planning community, right from workforce planning experts to managers, through various education activities and networking opportunities. SWPP acts as a great source of industry expertise, tools, trends, e-learning and traditional training programs, and many more benefits.

Appendix B—Useful Resources

I am not recommending or endorsing any of these resources. All I am trying to do is getting you started on the road to understanding call center dynamics. This is not an exhaustive list but just a snapshot of the various learning material and useful resources available for further reading and study.

A. Useful information on call center training, best practices and community events can be found at the following website: www.icmi.com

B. For unique insights on customer relationship management, visit www.crmxchange.com

C. Certain assorted links that are a great source of information about call centers are www.the-resource-center.com and www.callcenterbasics.com

D. Blogs, Expert Advice, White Papers and much more—you name it and you will find it at http://searchcrm.techtarget.com

E. Trade publications like Call Center Focus and Call Center Magazine are a great way of keeping abreast of the latest happenings on the call center horizon.

F. The Internet is a storehouse of information resources and community sites on call centers so log on and bookmark the relevant websites.

References

2010 Call Center Outlook Survey Results.

Accenture Research.

American Management Association Study.

AMR Research.

Babcock, P. (2004). *Shedding light on knowledge management*. HRMagazine, 49(5), 46-50.

Barker, R.L. (2003). The social work dictionary (5th Ed.). Washington, DC: NASW Press.

British Call Center Association.

Forrester Research Report 2009: *Obstacles To Customer Experience Success.*

Frost & Sullivan: Assessment of the Asia Pacific Contact Center Market Report.

Gartner: www.gartner.com/it/page.jsp?id=1423413

International Data Corporation Report 2011: *Worldwide and U.S. Outsourced Customer Care Services* 2011-15 *Forecast.*

John, M. (2002). *3.3 Million US Services Jobs To Go Offshore.* Forrester Research.

Macmillan Dictionary: www.macmillandictionary.com/dictionary/british/call-centre

Magic Quadrant for CRM Customer Service Contact Centers. Gartner RAS Core Research Note G00212151, Michael Maoz, 15 April 2011, R3620 04222012.

McKinsey and Company Report.

NASSCOM-Mckinsey Study 2005: *Extending the leadership of the Indian IT and BPO industries.*

Norling, P. (2001). *Call Center Companies and New Patterns of Organization.* Economic and Industrial Democracy. 22: pp. 155-58.

Offshoring Opportunities Amid Economic Turbulence—The A.T. Kearney Global Services Location Index™, 2011.

Oxford English Dictionary:
http://oxforddictionaries.com/search?searchType=dictionary&isWritersandEditors=true&searchUri=All&q=care&searchBtn=Search&contentVersion=WORLD

PC Magazine Encyclopedia:

www.pcmag.com/encyclopedia term/0,2542,t= call+center&i= 39218,00.asp

U.S. Bureau of Labor Statistics: Customer Service Representatives. Occupational Outlook Handbook, 2010-11 Edition.

Yankee Group (www.yankeegroup.com).